MW00387579

A
Compendium
of
Common
Knowledge

A
Compendium
of
Common
Knowledge
1558–1603

Elizabethan Commonplaces
for Writers, Actors & Re-enactors

Maggie Secara

Los Angeles

A Compendium of Common Knowledge 1558–1603:
Elizabethan Commonplaces for Writers, Actors & Re-enactors

Popinjay Press
Los Angeles, California
popinjay@elizabethan.org

© 1990–2008 Maggie Secara. All rights reserved.

Available online from www.elizabethan.org

Please address all comments, questions, and requests or suggestions for additional topics to maggiros@elizabethan.org

All images are in the public domain with the exception of the following drawings, which are copyright Paula Kate Marmor and used by permission of the artist: map of England in the 1500s, page 5; map of Ireland in the 1500s, page 66; Ingatestone Hall plan, page 153.

Much of the material in this book was previously published on the elizabethan.org website designed by Paula Kate Marmor.

Manufactured in the United States of America

ISBN: 978-0-9818401-0-9

LCCN: 2008905481

Design and composition: www.dmargulis.com

This little book belongs particularly to

The Guild of St. George R P F *'86 –'91*

The Ren Faire History Snobs Tribe, 2008

and

Katie Marmor

Contents

vii

A
Compendium
of
Common
Knowledge

Short Attention Span History

*The countess of Southampton's
wedding picture*

T HIS book is not a series of essays or articles. It is bites of Elizabethan life that are, have been, or should be common knowledge for those of us who work and play in the 16ᵗʰ century on a regular basis: the little things that make up daily life, that everyone knows without thinking. It is primarily social history, not political or military. It is neither exhaustive nor comprehensive, but it is what the Elizabethans know and do, present tense.

This little book has been through a lot of changes. It has been circulated a few pages at a time, in sections, in whole, and in part through three large Renaissance Faires, and any number of smaller ones. Since blossoming on the Internet, it has been used in classrooms on three continents. People recite parts of it in my hearing, unaware that they are using my words. Parts of it turn up verbatim and unattributed, sometimes re-arranged, on other people's websites and guild guidelines. That's okay. That's what it's for: to establish and circulate a base of common knowledge about the Elizabethan age for people who need it.

The way I see it, if you learn even one new thing in a day, you're ahead. The layout of this little book always was designed to make that one new thing immediate, interesting, and accessible. It predates the World Wide Web by a few years, but it might have been designed with the Internet in mind. And now it has returned to hardcopy so it can be used in workshops, stashed in a basket, flipped through, marked up, dog-eared, and highlighted. And learned from.

Be sure to check the website at www.elizabethan.org for additions and updates.

A note on notes Where are the footnotes? There aren't any. Much of this book was collected over a long stretch of courses, workshops, conversations, random reading, books, and articles. Some things can be found in any basic volume on Elizabethan history. Some are the colorful but irrelevant things you read while researching something else. Besides, if I had footnoted every fact, it might have doubled the size of the book, and made reading in bed potentially life threatening. Where possible, I've added principal sources to many pages, using the author's name and the title in alphabetical order. Refer to the Bibliography for complete information. Everything is in there somewhere.

Honours and graces In the years since this little project has been on the Internet, many real-world changes have come about, faires and guilds come and gone, friends lost and friends found. While any errors of fact or interpretation are mine and mine alone, the information here comes from my own research and that of many others.

Most particularly, I am indebted to the following people for providing either questions or answers at significant times: Kevin Brown, Lloyd Winter, Walter Nelson, Malcolm Scott, Nan Earnheart, Stephen Gillan, and Jeff Bissiri. Also Gereg Jones Muller, Luis Rodriguez, Donna Moran, Fred Louaillier, Rory Downward, Cathleen & James Myers, Terri Saffouri, John Hertz, and the late Dr. Ron Love. Not to forget Jess Miller, Cecily Thompson, Paul Giles, Linda Abrams, Jerry & Judy Gorelick, Elizabeth Pruyne, Angie Grimes, Dr. Ari Berk, and Alan Chudnow.

The greatest debt is to my friend, Kate Marmor, who first proposed the web effort that has become this volume, and has encouraged, inspired, and asked new questions, dug up or created the art, and designed beautiful pages for the entire site at elizabethan.org.

And finally special gratitude is owed to Ron and Phyllis Patterson for giving us all a place to play and providing the basis for a lifetime's research project.

North Hollywood, California
Spring 2008

Philosophical Introduction

T H E past is not all the same place. This is important.
For that matter, the Renaissance is not the same thing
from beginning to end. So it seems important to point out right
now, up front, that this little bit of the Renaissance under discussion here is not the Middle Ages and is not the Baroque. It
is also not the Quintecento in Florence or Venice. It is England
in the time of Elizabeth, with a trailing edge of Tudor. I have
tried very hard to keep all references, and even all the illustra-
tions, firmly within that range. If I can't be sure that people in
her time knew or used a thing, better to leave it out.

As writers and particularly as actors (or re-enactors), we often speak of the past in the present tense. Not because we can't
tell the difference between then and now, or even because we
wish to have lived then, but because while we're doing it, we
need this information to be real and immediate and everyday.
For us, the past is very present indeed. And when we gig in per-
sona, or write dialog, or develop a scene, it is useless to speak of
what they did, when we need our audience to understand *what
they do*. Which is why, you will notice, this little book is presented more or less entirely in the present tense.

On the faire circuit we often say that we are playing a chapter
of history, not a page. It's a very big chapter, and lots of things
change, but not the legal age for marriage. In '99 as in '58, pennies are made of silver, and 12 pennies make a shilling. Gentlemen put their servants in livery, but the army (such as it is)
does not. Peers cannot be arrested for anything except felony,
treason, and breach of the peace. Turnips are on the common
man's menu while potatoes are rumored to be poisonous. The

world is composed of Air, Earth, Fire, and Water, and Judgment Day awaits us all.

God Saue the Quene

England in the 1500s

Services & Occupations

You get...	From the...
Books	Stationer or bookseller
Cloth	Mercer
Hats	Milliner or hatter
Suit of clothes	Tailor
Shirts/smocks	Seamstress
Ready made clothes	Draper
Arrows	Fletcher

A Tailor at Work

You get...	From the...
Bows	Bowyer
Horseshoes	Farrier
Other iron work	Blacksmith
Armor	Armourer
A portrait	Limner
Legal service	Lawyer
Drugs, etc.	Apothecary
Dentistry	Barber surgeon

In the city...

A stapler	Buys and sells raw wool; also silk and linen.
A draper	Deals in cloth (wholesale), plus some ready-made garments and dry goods.
A mercer	Is the cloth retailer: the local fabric store is a mercer's shop. One may be a silk mercer or a wool mercer, and so on.

In your own household, your...

Man of business	Is your accountant, looks after your investments.
Steward	Oversees the running of your estates.
Factor	Does business for you in London, or in another country.
Nurse	Takes care of infants and young children.
Wet nurse	Breastfeeds the baby (maybe as long as the first 2 years) .
Tutor	Educates your children.

Some Numbers, Measures & Hours

T HE *metric system* has not been invented yet, so don't use it.

+ Land is measured in acres.
+ Beer comes in pints and is stored in gallons.
+ Distance is measured in miles, feet, and inches.

Counting up

Teenage numbers are as we use them now: sixteen, seventeen, etc. Never say ten-and-six to mean 16. Nor six-and-ten, for that matter.

Numbers are correctly expressed in "long" form only after age 20. That is, you are one-and twenty (21) or five-and-thirty (35) but never thirty-and-five.

Reckoning the time

Clock time may be expressed either as:

+ Two o'clock (yes, really)
+ Two of the clock
+ Half past 2 (or quarter past)
+ The bawdy hand of the dial is now upon the prick of noon!

Numbers are frequently written in lower case Roman numerals, with the last "i" in a number written as a "j", such as *vij* for 7.

Reckoning the date

While the rest of Europe went over to the Gregorian calendar in the 12th century, England refuses to give up the Julian date, even though it is clearly "off". We will not submit to the Popish plot to steal 10 days from the calendar God gave us until 1752.

This leads to historical confusion when an event, such as the

Armada, is known to be taking place on a particular date in England and 10 days later in Spain—at the same time.

For the first three months of any year, we are also not entirely sure what year it is. The legal or civil year begins on March 25, Lady Day, which is also a quarter day. But everyone knows that New Year's Day is January 1.

This leads to events in January, February, and most of March being recorded with a stroke or slash. The earl and countess of Southampton, for example, were married on 19 February 1566/67. That is, legally it was still 1566, but for calculating anniversaries, it was already 1567.

New year's gifts are exchanged on January 1.

Hutton: *Stations of the Sun*   *Sources*
Emmison: *Tudor Secretary*
Baldwin: *The Elizabethan World*

Games

DRINKING may be done in taverns, alehouses, or tippling houses.

Gambling is *gaming* (game-ing).
Playing at dice is *dicing*.

A popular dice game is Hazard, *At the table* played rather like Craps.

The word for backgammon is *tables*. The "ace-deuce" version is called *the Corsican game.*

You can lose a good deal of money in a *tabling den*.

An easy card game is Landsknecht. Two much harder ones are Primero and Taroccho (ta-ro'-koh), played with tarot cards.

Other sport   A whorehouse or *stew* is also a *bawdy house* or a *leaping house* or a *shugging den*.

A *drab* is a woman of low character or a prostitute. A *drabber* is someone who spends too much time with such women.

A *punk* is a whore who may work in a *stew*. Working girls in Southwark in the domain of the Bishop of Winchester are also called *Winchester geese*.

NOTE: Scottish money is worth about one-quarter of the English in the same denominations. That is, a Scottish pound is worth about five English shillings. Irish money is worth even less, and they may want to pay you in nails. (Be wary when gaming with either.)

Money: What You Need to Know

The basics   ALL coins are silver or gold, including the pennies.
In times not too long past, copper was used to extend (debase) the coinage without actually spending any more silver. But no money is actually minted as a copper coin. If someone gives you a modern copper penny, laugh and tell him to come back with some real money.

There is also no paper money. You cannot, for example, have a 5-pound note.

The basic denominations are *pounds, shillings,* and *pence.*

12 pence make a shilling

20 shillings make a pound

In writing, the abbreviation for:
penny is *d*
shilling is *s*
pound is £

A *sovereign* is a gold coin worth 1 pound (but try to think of it as *The coins in* 20 shillings). There is no coin called a "pound" until after 1583, *your pocket* although that is the basic monetary unit.

The *angel* is one of the most common gold coins in circulation. An angel is worth 10 shillings (½ pound). You would never say you owed somebody 6 angels. But you might say you gave your servant an angel to spend at the faire. To coerce someone's servant, you might suggest that the sweet voice of an angel would convince him.

The *crown* is the most common coin in circulation. Worth 5 shillings, it is issued in both gold and silver.

The crown is also equal to a *Venetian ducat*, a *Flemish gelder*, or a *French êcu* (sometimes called a *French crown*). A *half-crown* is worth 2 shillings 6 pence (sometimes expressed as "2 and 6").

The *shilling* is a silver coin worth 12d.

The *sixpence* is a silver coin worth six pence.

A *groat* is a silver coin worth 4 pence.

The *penny* is a silver coin worth a penny (never a pence). You might have several pennies in your pocket, to the value of several pence.

A coin or value of 2 pence is called *tuppence*.

A half-penny is called a *ha'-penny* (not a ha'pence).

The *farthing* is a ¼-penny fragment so tiny as to be impractical, but still in circulation from less inflated times.

The *guinea* does not yet exist, and will not be minted till the late 17th century. Don't refer to it.

The *mark* is "money of account". That is, it is a value worth ⅔ of a pound (13s 4d) but there is no coin worth that amount in the 16th century. It is often used in high-level transactions, such as selling land, figuring feudal fines, or calculating dowries.

Spending In practice, people seldom speak of ordinary amounts of money in terms of pounds, unless it is in thousands, like the annual value of an estate, or a special "voluntary" tax.

You probably think of ordinary, daily expenses in terms of shillings and pence. ("I lost 30 shillings last night at tables.")

Money bought more in those days. Do not just substitute pounds for dollars. Try using shillings, or even pennies, depending on the item.

Thirty pounds for a pair of gloves is highway robbery. But 30 shillings for a pair of gloves doesn't sound so bad, at least theatrically speaking. (Actually 7 shillings is closer to the truth, unless they are finely decorated.)

For smaller items, like food and drink, use pennies. A penny or two for a pot of ale is about right, where 2 pounds or even 2 shillings is unthinkable.

Tip a household servant no more than a few pence. Remember, he only makes £2–£5 per year! That tip is called a *vail*. A common vail is about a penny.

If you're buying information or a favor from anybody besides a servant use gifts instead of money. For servants—use money.

Religion

EVERYONE has one. We were all brought up to be Christians of one sort or another. If you were born before 1555, or so, your parents were Catholic. Until later in the reign, it's safe to say your grandparents were Catholic.

The official established state religion is the Church of England. It is referred to as the *new religion* or the *established church*, but not as "C of E". (Do not give in to the modern inclination to acronyms.)

Everyone is required to attend a church service once a month. *Rituals* The service is referred to as the Prayer Service, or the Prayer Book Service, and sometimes as Common Prayer, Holy Eucharist, or the Lord's Supper.

Mass is a Catholic service only. It is illegal to hold or attend one at any time in the reign, though punishment varies. People of high rank are less likely to get in trouble.

Older people may still refer to the service as a Mass, but it is politically touchy. Reformers refer to the detestable enormities of the "Mass priests".

The *rosary* is period in several forms, including the modern one, and used only by Catholics. The rosary cross usually does not include a *corpus*, or figure of Christ.

Being a Roman Catholic is not a crime, but there is a fine for *Catholics* not conforming to the established religion; that is, for not going to church on Sunday. And every church is a protestant church.

Paying the fine *does not* allow you to have a priest or practice the Catholic faith. There is no legal way for Catholics to practice their faith.

It is illegal to be a Catholic priest in England. It is *very* illegal to be a Jesuit, since Jesuits are assumed to be traitors.

A non-conforming Catholic is called a *recusant* (rec-you-zant) and is guilty of *recusancy*.

Protestants sometimes refer to Roman Catholics as *Romanists*. Catholics do not refer to themselves as Papists.

The Pope published a writ (1570) absolving English Catholics from allegiance to the Queen, since she is (he says) a heretic. Anyone who kills her is pre-absolved from the sin of murder.

Puritans The term *puritan* is common in period, although sometimes the word *precisionist* is used.

Puritanism is not a separate religion, but a Calvinist leaning within the Anglican church. Puritans do not yet look like Pilgrims.

Puritans in Scotland are Presbyterians and Congregationalists.

Everyone else You can apply the term *atheist* to anyone who disagrees with you in religion. In usage, it does not entirely mean you believe that there is no God, but that you don't believe in my God. Any heretic can be called an atheist. So can a Jew.

Language: Thee & Thou

THIS is not some special grammar you are taught in school, but simply the ordinary way people talk. Your excuse for incorrect usage cannot be that you were poorly educated.

Say:
  How art *thou*, never how are *thee*.
  What would*st thou* have of me?
  I will go *with thee*.
  Thou *art* a rogue.

When the next word begins with a vowel, use *thine* for *thy*.

Say:
  I like *thy* face.

but:
  I applaud *thine* effort.

The "-st" ending is only used with *thou* and only with verbs.

Say:
  Whither thou goest I will go.
  I did see him go with *thee*.

not:
  I didst see him

and never:
  I didst see-eth him

The "-eth" ending is only used with he, she, and it.

Say:
  He *loveth* best that *loveth* well.
  God *knoweth* why!

Thou and *thee* are familiar or informal forms of *you*. You use it   *Using* thou
to address your children, your servants, your wife, your most   *familiarly*
intimate friends, your dog, and God. (Hey, who knows you
better than God?)

Use the more formal *you* when addressing your parents,
your master, your social superiors, your patron, your custom-
ers, your officers, and your horse, who may be worth as much
as you are.

The familiar and formal forms (*thou* and *you*) get mixed in
a sentence even in Shakespeare. But only downward or to an
equal, never up.

That is, you might address your servant using both thou and
you together, but he wouldn't do that to you. Anger and strong
feeling, of course, cancel other conventions.

Still, his lordship may take offense if his tenant chats him up
using "thou", or he may simply ignore it, but you never know!

Love & Marriage

I T is generally considered foolish to marry for love, although love may occur in marriage.

Your parents and friends are better equipped than you are to look out for your best interests, being mature and experienced in the world. Let them negotiate and recommend and you're much more likely to be happy in marriage.

Just because a marriage is arranged doesn't mean you've never met the other person. Except among the lofty nobility, most people arrange their children's marriages with the children of neighbors and friends.

The lower on the social scale you are, the more likely you are to have a choice in the matter.

Exemplary (and disastrous) love matches: Robert Dudley and Amy Robsart; Lord Darnley and Mary Queen of Scots; Edward earl of Oxford and Anne Cecil.

Rare successful love matches: the 7th Baron and Lady Berkeley; the 2nd Earl of Bedford and his 3rd countess.

Everyone wants (and expects) to have children.   *Children*

Children are the property of their parents, and give them the respect a servant gives his master. Or else.

Wives are the property of their husbands. *See previous*   *Wives*
admonition.

Some women are more independent than others, and some fear marriage. However, every woman expects to be married, and to depend on her male relatives throughout her life.

Of course, not everyone is in a hurry to get married, but marriage means being in charge of your own home.

Women who would have been drawn to convent life in the old days no longer have that option, and must either marry or be a burden to their families.

Widows can own property and run their own businesses.   *Widows*

A widow is entitled to ⅓ of her husband's estates (after the bills are paid), if he has heirs. All of it if he does not. This "widow's third" is separate from and in addition to her *jointure*.

It is still considered a good idea to re-marry to protect one's interests, however, and the interests of minor children.

Since there are tedious problems to do with whether a woman's word or signature is legally binding, she really must have a husband.

If she doesn't, her friends will worry about her being taken advantage of by sharp servants. This worry increases if she wants to marry one of them.

In general, every man wants to marry too, or at least acknowl-   *Men*
edges that he must.

If he is not noble, he must be married to become the legal head of a household and eligible to hold public or ecclesiastical office and other positions of civic responsibility.

When he is widowed, a man also looks to remarry, especially if he has children. The traditional waiting period is a *month's mind*. To marry again after a month is not considered hasty.

Divorce is actually more difficult to obtain in the protestant regime than in the Catholic, even with cause. Since you can't apply to the Pope anymore, you have to get an Act of Parliament! That's a lot more people to buy.

Sources   Cressy: *Birth, Marriage, and Death*
Duffy: *Voices of Morebath*
Pearson: *Elizabethans at Home*

Betrothal & Wedding

WITH parental permission, boys are legal to marry at 14, girls at 12, though it is not recommended so early. One comes of age at 21.

Sir Thomas More recommended that girls not marry before 18 and boys not before 22.

In non-noble families, the most common age for marriage is 25–26 for men, about 23 for women. This is because it's best to wait until you can afford a home and children. Also, most apprenticeships don't end until the mid 20s.

Noble families may arrange marriage much earlier. Robert Dudley's sister Katherine, who became the countess of Huntingdon, did go to the altar at age 7, but that was extraordinary.

When the participants are very young, it is principally to secure a dynastic alliance. They generally do not live together as man and wife (by any definition). Often, the bride may go to live with the groom's family to be brought up in domestic management by her mother-in-law.

Marriage is a contract that begins with a *betrothal*. *The*

At a betrothal, the two people join hands. He gives her a *contract*
ring to be worn on the right hand. It changes to the left at the
wedding.

They seal the contract with a kiss, and signatures.

A marriage contract includes provision both for the bride's
dowry and for a *jointure*, or *settlement*, in cash and property by
the husband's family, which guarantees her welfare should her
husband die first.

If he breaks the marriage contract without good cause, he
has to give back any tokens or gifts received.

Betrothals can be terminated by mutual consent. In certain
circumstances, one can withdraw unilaterally if a long separa-
tion has occurred between them, or if the other is:

* Guilty of heresy or apostasy (conversion or re-conversion
  to Rome)
* Guilty of infidelity
* Seriously disfigured
* Proved to be previously (and still) married or contracted
  to marry
* Guilty of enmity or wickedness or drunkenness

A proper wedding is based on three things: consent, exchange of tokens (such as the ring) and consummation. It can
be annulled only if it is not consummated.

It is luckiest to have the wedding in the morning.

Bridesmaids see to the floral decorations, make little flower *Weddings*
bouquets as favors for the guests, and make the garland.

The wedding *garland* should be rosemary and roses. Rosemary represents love and fidelity.

The bride carries her garland till after the ceremony, then wears it on her head.

The father of the bride usually pays for the festivities, including favors or small gifts to everyone. Common gifts include ribbons, gloves, and scarves. According to Machyn's Diary, James Sutton gave away 100 pairs of gloves when his daughter was married in 1559.

On changing names The bride takes her husband's family name on marriage.

In some deeply rural communities, however, women and men alike are still known as much by their occupation or location as by surname. Lucy Baines who lives at River Farm becomes "Lucy at River" in the parish record. When John Baines buys the mill, he may become known as John Miller.

Where there are many families of the same surname, wives may also be known by their husband's first or first and last name. Adam Tychy's wife Bridget could become Bridget Adam or Bridget Adam Tychy as well as Bridget Tychy. (This is a common form in the Germanies as well.)

Sources Cressy: *Birth, Marriage, and Death*
Duffy: *Voices of Morebath*
Jones: *Elizabethan Age*
Orlin: *Elizabethan Households*
Pearson: *Elizabethans at Home*

Comparative Religion: Roman Catholics

THIS *is a selection only of the principal attributes of the Roman Catholic faith as understood in period. It is by no means complete, but in general covers the points on which the*

Lutherans and other protestants disagree with Rome in the 16th century.

Salvation is gained through faith in God, the prayers of the Church, the grace of the sacraments, and doing good works. Good works include both acts of mercy and major church building projects.

Only the Church, through its priests, can interpret God's will to Man. The laity do not read the Bible for themselves.

The source of the Church's authority is *Scripture*, the divinely inspired writings of the Church Fathers, and an amorphous thing called *Sacred Tradition*.

The seven *sacraments* are: Baptism, Confirmation, Holy Eucharist, Penance, Extreme Unction, Holy Orders, and Matrimony. *Grace* is conferred by a sacrament simply from your participation in it, and your faith in its power.

The *Pope*, as the rightful heir of St. Peter, is the head of the Church. He is considered to be infallible in matters of faith and morals, although this is not yet dogma.

There is a half-way point between Heaven and Hell called *Purgatory*, where a person's sins are purged to make him worthy of Heaven. The prayers of the living can shorten a soul's stay in Purgatory, so it is good to pray for the dead.

The saints were more virtuous than they needed to be to get into Heaven, so there is a kind of reserve of leftover grace available. Drafts on this reserve are called *indulgences*, and they are for sale—or they were before Henry VIII put a stop to it.

The saints are Mankind's advocates before God the Father. *Worship* is directed to God but prayers are often addressed to one of the saints.

The Blessed Virgin *Mary* is the most revered holy personage who is not actually divine. The Mother of God is thought to be more compassionate than the sternly just Father. Churches called Saint Mary's are named for her.

All *rituals*, simple or elaborate, are carried out in Latin.

Priests cannot marry, and are required to remain celibate.

More Language: Some random vocabulary

WHEN you talk about having a tooth pulled at the dentist's, say you have had it *drawn* by the *barber* or *barber surgeon*.

When we refer to *corn*, we are referring, mainly, to barley. If not barley, then it is whatever the major grain crop in the region is (rye is common). It is never corn-on-the-cob or maize.

Englishmen speak of living *in* a particular street instead of *on* it. Shakespeare lived for a time in a house in Silver Street, or one knows a tailor with a shop in the High Street.

Where American towns have a Main Street, the main drag in an English town of any size is usually called the High Street. There are also regional variations, such as Fore Street or Silver Street.

A *village* is likely to be built around a *village green* and may not have a street running into or through it at all.

If traffic actually does run nearby, you might say that children were playing in the *lane* or the *road*.

You can call a doll a *poppet*. You can call a child a poppet too. *Sweeting* is a pet name both for lovers and for children.

Comparative Religion:
The Church of England

F OR our purposes, most of these basically Lutheran tenets apply to all protestants. The Calvinist ("puritan") refinements
are presented further along.

Man's wickedness is so great that no amount of good works
could hope to atone for our *sin*. God, being all good, would not
require something of us that is impossible. Therefore, the only
thing necessary for salvation is believing in His Name ("*justifi-
cation by faith*").

The Church exists to guide but is not necessary for *salvation*.
There is no need for priests to interpret God's will. Supporting
the Church, or denying the flesh, does not bring you closer to
God. If you are united with Him at all, it is completely and
absolutely.

The Roman church has corrupted the original doctrines and
teachings of Christ and his apostles for its own purpose, and
no longer represents the true faith of Christ. The only source
of religious *authority* is Scripture.

The two *sacraments* are Baptism and Holy Eucharist (Com-
munion). The other so-called sacraments are worthy but not
Scripturally justified.

No sacrament is efficacious without understanding and
faith.

There is no principle of papal authority: the *Pope* (or Anti-
christ) is just a man and subject to error. He is not the leader of
the true church.

The doctrine of *Purgatory* is denied as being un-Scriptural.
You go straight to Heaven or Hell, according to God's judg-

ment. Thus prayers for the dead, including Masses and pur-
chased indulgences, are of no value. To pray for the dead is
heretical.

The selling of *indulgences* is a particular vice because a) it
is not supported in Scripture and b) it encourages sin. The
Church cannot put divine forgiveness up for sale.

Your relation to God is not mediated by priests or saints, but
is a personal acceptance of the message of Scripture.

The Virgin Mary almost disappears from protestant con-
sciousness, and the role of the saints is greatly diminished.

All rituals are performed in the vernacular (English). Rituals are less elaborate, although candles and church bells are still
in use.

Ministers can marry, although the Queen would prefer they
did not.

Titles & Forms of Address

EVEN *small children know how to address their social
superiors.*

Sir goes only with a man's given name. To address a knight
using only his surname, say *Master* (see examples below).

Lord implies a peerage whether temporal (baron or better)
or spiritual (bishops).

Not every knight is a lord; not every lord is a knight. It is best
not to say *my lord* to anyone not so entitled.

A *territorial title* is one which is attached to a particular piece
of land, such as a county.

Peers sign their names and refer to themselves and each
other by their territorial titles, such as "Henry Southampton",
"Francis Bedford", or "Thomas Rutland".

Captain Sir Walter Ralegh

Every woman married to a knight or better can be called *my lady*. For unmarried women, see the various examples.

The children of a knight, baron, or viscount have no titles at all other than Master and Mistress.

All the sons of a marquis or a duke are styled *lord*.

Only the eldest son of an earl is called *lord* (because he takes his father's secondary title and is one, by courtesy) though all an earl's daughters are styled *lady*. They retain this courtesy even if they marry a commoner.

Your Grace belongs properly only to royal blood: the queen, dukes, and visiting princesses. It does not apply to earls or countesses in the 16th century. Archbishops share this honor as princes of the church.

The styles of *Honourable* or *Right Honourable* for younger sons and daughters of peers has not yet come into use. Peers, however, often receive dedications in a form such as "the right Honourable the Lord Chandos".

Esquires are the younger sons of peers, the heirs male of knights, esquires of the body, and officials such as judges, sheriffs, and officers of the royal household.

Esquire is not a title, and it is used only after a gentleman's surname; as, William More, Esquire.

If you are not noble, you may wish to address those above you as *Your Worship, Your Honour,* or *Your Lordship/Ladyship.*

Children are taught to address their parents as *Sir* and *Madam,* or *my lord* and *my lady.* A noble child refers to *my lady mother* and *the lord my father.*

Direct address

PEERS

Francis Russell, the Earl of Bedford can be called
    Lord Bedford,
        but *not* Lord Russell
        and *not* Lord Francis.
Thomas Howard, Viscount Bindon can be called
    Lord Bindon,
        but *not* Lord Howard
        and *not* Lord Thomas.
Sir William Cecil, Baron Burghley, the Lord Treasurer can be called
    Sir William (before his elevation to the peerage) or
    Lord Burghley or
    My Lord Treasurer,
        but *not* Sir Cecil.
Margaret Stewart, the Countess of Lennox, whose maiden name was Douglas, can be called
    Lady Lennox or

Lady Margaret
> but *not* Lady Douglas
> and *is never styled* Margaret Douglas Lady Stuart, Countess of Lennox.

Jane, the Baroness Lumley, is a baron's wife. Her maiden name was Fitzalan. She can be called
Lady Lumley
> but *not* Lady Fitzalan
> and *is never styled* Jane Fitzalan Lady Lumley.

Mary Wriothesley, the dowager countess of Southampton can be called
my lady countess or
Lady Southampton
> even after her re-marriage to Sir Thomas Heneage.
> In letters she sometimes appears as "my old lady South-ampton", to tell her from the new one, her son's wife.

Usage note: A woman takes her husband's name at marriage, and leaves her father's name behind. The apparent custom of using the lady's maiden name as if she had never changed it comes from the historian's need to differentiate one countess of Bedford from another, and to emphasize family connections. It is not Elizabethan usage.

Knightly Rank

Sir John Packington can be called
Sir John or
Master Packington,
> but not Sir Packington.

Captain Sir Walter Raleigh can also be called
Sir Walter or
Master Raleigh or

Captain Raleigh,
> but never Sir Raleigh.

Sir Thomas Jermyn's wife Catherine, whose maiden name was Killigrew, can be called

Lady Jermyn or
Dame Catherine
> but *not* Lady Catherine
> and *not* Catherine Killigrew Lady Jermyn.

Usage note: The designation Dame appears to be applied to the Christian name of a knight's lady or the surname of a citizen's or burgess's wife or widow. Later it will be used for female members of knightly orders, but there aren't any of those in this reign.

Courtesy titles: maids of honour and other unmarried children

Courtesy titles are used only with Christian names, never with surnames. Use the following samples as guidelines.

Maids of honour

Lady Margaret Russell, a maid of honour and an earl's daughter can be called

Lady Margaret Russell *or*
Mistress Russell,
> but never Lady Russell
> and is *never ever* styled "Lady Margaret Mistress Russell".

Margaret Radcliffe, a maid of honour who is a knight's daughter, should be called

Mistress Margaret or
Mistress Radcliffe,
> but not Lady Margaret (a Royal Household office does not confer a title).

CHILDREN OF PEERS

George Paulet, the Marquis of Winchester's second son, is
Lord George or
Master Paulet (but this sort of familiarity may be
insulting)
but never Lord Paulet.
Elizabeth Cecil, the Baron Burghley's daughter, can be
Mistress Elizabeth, or
Mistress Cecil
but *neither* Lady Elizabeth *nor* Lady Cecil.

Masters & Servants

G ROOMS are generic household serving men: grooms of   *Terminology*
the stable, chamber, etc. Females of the same order are
called maids or serving maids: of the kitchen, chamber, still
room, etc.

Most of the servants in any large household are men, includ-ing the cooks.

Personal attendant is a descriptive term, not a job title. In rehearsal, it separates everyone else's personal servants (of all ranks) from household grooms and maids.

USAGE NOTE: *Never introduce anyone as "my P.A."* This was a term commonly used in some Renaissance faires c.1975–1995. While I am assured that it has fallen out of fashion, it may at any time rear its awkward head again. Don't let this happen.

The term *valet* is in use in English as early as 1567. According to the OED, a valet is "a man-servant performing duties chiefly relating to the person of his master; a gentleman's personal attendant."

From *varlet*, the British pronunciation is (and almost cer-tainly was) "val'-ett". Valet (val-ay') is a little too French, don't y'think?

The most common term for the job is *manservant*, or just *man*. For example, in Romeo and Juliet, Benvolio refers to Romeo's ever present servant as "his man", as in "Romeo came not home tonight. I spoke with his man."

Female equivalents are *waiting gentlewoman* or *maid*, de-pending on the rank and duties of the relevant parties. A lady might refer to her gentlewoman or her maid. Only the Queen has ladies in waiting.

As a verb, say that you *serve*, or *wait upon*, or *attend* (but not "work for") someone. Or that you are waited on or attended by someone.

General attitudes   Credit, or reputation, has to do with one's personal dignity or honour. Frances countess of Sussex once said (1588) "My credit is more to me than my life."

A servant and master strive to do each other credit. As a lady of quality, it is unbecoming to your dignity to carry your own shopping basket. As her servant, it is unbecoming to your dignity to let her.

As a gentleman, it befits your dignity to dress yourself and your servants well. As a servant, you do your master credit by looking and behaving well. Sir Thomas Smith said, "A gentleman should go like a gentleman."

People do not dress their servants in rags.

Servants are not democrats. In general, they approve of the social order, just like their masters. And they intend to take advantage of it.

A servant in a fine house expects (if he is clever) to rise in the world, improve his fortunes, and create an even better place for his children. A stable groom might aspire to become butler or steward in the same or a greater house. The pot boy might hope one day to be chief cook.

Servants will take money from anyone. They will accept a *vail* (tip) for any service rendered. ("Here's a penny to drink my health.") Or a *douceur* (sweetener) for favors requested. They expect to be vailed for delivering a gift or message. Their masters are aware of this, and do it themselves to other people's servants. It all evens out.

It is not considered dishonest unless loyalties become confused and compromised.

The good servant, like a good waiter, is attentive. The best servant is a little bit psychic. He is there when you need him but never hovers. He finds some virtuous occupation when you disappear. He is neither lewd nor vain, but maintains a respectable countenance, to the credit of his master. He is modest but never craven, humble but never base, candid but not insolent.

The good master is proud but never despotic. He is patient,

governing his household with fatherly care. He does not twist your sincere desire to serve into a sincere desire to punch him out. He lets you do your job. He maintains his superior station, as God has given it him, by honourable behavior, not by argument or blows.

Sources Scott: *Book of Orders and Rule*
Stone: *Crisis of the Aristocracy*

Patronage: Retinue, Companions & Livery

Men YOUNG men go to Court to find a patron. Any of the great noblemen draws such gentlemen to him in an essentially feudal relationship, based on personal loyalty, service, gifts, and favors.

These can include knights and younger sons, often with substantial incomes of their own. They might instead be scholars, musicians, and intellectuals, depending on his lordship's inclinations.

Some of the gentry put their sons into great homes for their education and advancement.

Retainers, companions, or waiting gentlemen are not necessarily poor relations. The Earl of Essex has a knight in his train worth £1,000 per year!

Some of these companions are the armed and often dangerous men who go everywhere with their patron, to back him in a quarrel or simply to be there for the party.

The lord maintains them, pays them a fee (wages or favors), puts them in his livery, and gives them nominal positions in the household.

Earl of Essex

Their main function is to increase the prestige of the patron while putting themselves in the way of advancement.

A noble lady draws her waiting women from her relatives (and *Women* her husband's) and the daughters of the local gentry.

She helps her unmarried girls of good family to find suitable marriages and introduces them at Court. If they marry any of the earl's followers, they may stay in attendance upon the countess.

A great lady's gentlewomen join her in sewing, minding the older children, dispensing charity in the neighborhood, nursing the household. They also take charge of her clothing, jewelry, etc.

The Queen's maids of honour are (or should be) in this same client relationship to the Queen. They are her servants; she looks after their future. She is supposed to be finding them good husbands.

Livery A nobleman provides livery for his servants in both summer and winter weights and sometimes variant colors. Sir William Petre put his household in blue for summer and a marbled grey for winter.

Livery can mean uniform clothing, or a badge of the lord's family on the sleeve, or a cloak in the lord's colors with the livery badge on the shoulder. The Earl of Southampton gave his followers each a gold chain as their livery token.

If you take a nobleman's livery—sometimes called *taking his cloth*—you become his follower (that is, his servant) and you owe him loyalty and other services as required.

You also share his exemption from certain laws. Peers cannot be arrested except for treason, felony, or breach of the peace, and neither can anyone in their livery. They cannot be put to torture without being attainted first.

A statute in every Tudor reign forbade the wearing of livery by any but household servants, to discourage factional fighting and the build up of private armies. For a while this threatened the freedom of liveried actors.

Sources Erickson: *The First Elizabeth*
Emmison: *Tudor Secretary*
The Lisle Letters, Muriel St. Clare Byrne, ed.
Orlin: *Elizabethan Households*
Rowse: *Shakespeare's Southampton*

Greasing the Wheels

THE sending and receiving of douceurs or gifts (never money!) in exchange for recent or future favors is common practice all through courtly society.

This is not considered corrupt. It's just the way things work. In fact, the system couldn't run without it.

There is no undue delicacy about defining what would be an acceptable gift, even to naming "a pretty dog" or a specific kind of hawk.

Quails are a prime delicacy, and can be used to sweeten a request, attract attention, or turn away wrath. (In the '40s, Lord Lisle bought them in large lots to give away a dozen at a time.)

You can send a gift just to let someone important know you're here, even without having a specific request or favor in mind. They'll owe you.

You may pass on a request from someone else. For example, one may say: "My friend, if you will send my lord of Leicester that hound of yours that he admired, he'll know it came from you and that I suggested it. He and I will both be in your debt, and he will be in mine." Get it?

Most frequent *douceur* (sweetener) type gifts include:

Game (often quail or deer)
Includes all game birds, such as herons, plovers, cranes, egrets, as well as cooked venison, boar's head, sturgeon, wild swine, salmon. May be cooked or caged, as appropriate.

Wine
The best wines are clarets from Gascony, though tastes differ.

Birds
All kinds of hawks are good. So are caged song birds, such as linnets.

Hunting dogs
Mastiffs, Talbot hounds, bloodhounds, coursing hounds, and so on.

Rare or special books
Manuscripts in Greek and Latin, translations from Arabic
and Hebrew, certain devotional texts.

Specialties
Also home made things like marmalade, beer, and honey.

Sources   Hartley: *Lost Country Life*
Rowse: *Life of the Society*
Stone: *Crisis of the Aristocracy*

A joiner at work

More Services & Occupations

NOTICE how many of these are also surnames:

You get...	From the...
Barrels	Cooper
Candles	Chandler
Gloves	Glover
Glass Windows	Glazier
Tile for the roof	Tiler
Leather goods	Saddler
Knives	Cutler
Furniture	Joiner

The...	Is...
Landlord	The man who runs the tavern, ale house, or ordinary.
Ostler	The man (or boy) in charge of the horses and stabling at an inn. Also stable boys and grooms, generally.
Fuller	The "dry-cleaner". Fulling is a process of beating cloth to plump and clean it.
Acater (uh-kay'-ter)	The agent you hire to order and buy food or goods you do not supply from your own estates. His name is the source of "caterer".
Warrener	The man who manages the rabbit warren and provides them to the table.

The...	Is...
Fowler	The man who manages the wildfowl population, nesting areas, and so forth on your estate, and supplies game birds for your table.
Cocker	The man who handles the birds at cockfighting.
Sawyer	The man you hire or contract with for sawn wooden planks (and so on) for building.
Turner	The person the joiner buys lathe-turned items from, such as table legs, finials, etc.

Domestic Details

WAINSCOTING is the full- or half-high wall paneling made of a series of vertical boards set together tongue and groove.

Paneling is wainscoting divided into squares by frames or other details.

When the ceiling is carved wood or fancy plaster work, divided into boxes or frames, it is a *coffered* ceiling.

In great houses the whole household eats in the *hall* or *great hall*. Most of the male servants sleep there on *pallets*, which are taken up during the day.

The family sits at the high table, and everyone else at *trestle* tables (sort of a board on saw horses) in order of household precedence.

The trestles in the hall are drawn (taken down) to make room for other things, like games, dancing, and sleeping room for most of the servants.

The private *dining parlour* or *dining chamber*, separate from the great hall, is a fairly new (that is, Tudor) innovation. His lordship's family is pulling itself away from communal living.

Privacy in general is rare and not much valued. Everybody shares a room and probably a bed. A household steward's job is not so much to see that all the staff or guests have rooms, but that "gentlemen should abide with other gentlemen, and the yeomen with yeomen."

The *solar* is her ladyship's bed-sitting room, always on the top floor, to catch as much daylight as possible for sewing.

The floor is probably covered with *rushes* just as in the Middle Ages. These must be turned and cleaned every so often. Nicer housewives in the later reign use rush mats instead of loose rushes. Extravagant and wealthy houses probably have some *Turkey carpets*.

If you do use rushes, you also make sure to strew *herbs* and flowers among them to mask the other smells of the house. Popular herbs for this purpose are:

Basil	Marjoram	Balm
Mawdelin	Chamomile	Pennyroyal
Cowslips	Rose petals	Daisies
Red mint	Sweet fennel	Sage
Germander	Tansey	Hops
Violets	Lavender	Winter savory
Lavender spike	Lavender cotton	

Emmison: *Tudor Secretary*   *Sources*
Harrison: *A Description of England*
Orlin: *Elizabethan Households*
Scott: *Book of Orders and Rules*

Of Bread & Wine

> The situation of our region, lying near unto the north, doth
> cause the heat of our stomachs to be of somewhat greater force:
> therefore our bodies do crave a little more ample nourishment
> than the inhabitants of the hotter regions are accustomed
> withal, whose digestive force is not altogether so vehement, be-
> cause their internal heat is not so strong as ours, which is kept
> in by the coldness of the air that from time to time (especially
> in winter) doth environ our bodies.
> —Wm. Harrison, *Description of England*, 1577

Bread THESE qualities of bread were commonly baked at Ingatestone Hall in the 1550s.

Manchet (pronounced man'-chett)
   A very fine white bread made from wheat flour.

Cheat
   A wheaten bread with the coarsest part of the bran
   removed.

Ravelled cheat
   A kind of cheat with more bran left in.

Bread is baked up by the *cast*, a batch of 2–3 loaves.

Harrison says that one bushel of flour produces 40 cast of
manchet, of which every loaf weighs 8 ounces going into the
oven and 6 coming out.

The ravelled cheat is generally made so that out of one bushel
of meal, (after two and twenty pounds of bran be sifted and
taken from it), they make thirty cast, every loaf weighing 18
ounces into the oven, and 16 ounces out. This makes a "brown
household bread agreeable enough for laborers."

The gentle folk commonly eat wheaten bread. Their poorer neighbors often use only rye or barley. In very hard times, beans, peas and (shudder) oats may be used.

> Bring us in no browne bred, for that is made of bran,
> Nor bring us in no white bred, for therein is no gain,
> But bring us in good ale!

Ale barm, a by-product of the brewing process, is used in bread making as a leavening agent. The barm is the liquor from the active ferment on the top of the ale pot.

Most wines are sweet and rather heavy. They probably have to be strained before you want to drink them, and may still have solid bits floating in them. *Drink*

Sugar and spices ("cinnamon and ginger, nutmeg and clove") are often added to wine and even to beer.

Wines include Malmsey, Canary, Rhenish, Claret, Sack, and Sherry.

Rhenish
A German wine, and very strong.

Claret
A red wine from Gascony (southern France).

Canary
A white wine from the Canary Islands.

Sack
Comes from Spain, and is commonly drunk with sugar and spices. A kind of sherry.

Aqua vitae
Any strong spirit such as brandy.

Brandywine
A distilled wine.

Perry
A (very) slightly alcoholic pear cider.

Verjuice
A very sharp vinegar made from grapes; used for cooking or as a condiment.

Ale and beer
Both made of malted barley and flavorings. Beer is ale with hops added.

Measuring it out   A *tun* is equal to 2 butts (as in Malmsey) or 4 hogsheads (as in wine) or 252 gallons.
A *puncheon* equals 84 gallons.
A *runlet* is various smaller amounts.

Emmison, F.G., *Tudor Secretary*
Harrison: *A Description of England*
Hartley: *Lost Country Life*
Rubel: Correspondence

More Language: Mishandled Words

YOUR *use of old-fashioned words should make you sound old-fashioned, not ignorant. Notice these usages.*
Wherefore means *Why*.

Whyfor is a made up word. Use *wherefore* when you mean "why", and *where* when you mean "where". Juliet did not say "Whyfor art thou Romeo?", but that's what she meant.

Mayhap has no "s". Don't say "mayhaps". You're thinking of "perhaps". To avoid confusion, try *belike*.

Stay means "to wait". If you mean to say that someone is waiting for you, and you are late (or whatever), say: I am stayed for.

Ta'en is short for taken. Use it for to mean "mistaken for". As in:

I fear thou hast ta'en me for someone else.

My brother is oft ta'en for me and I for him.

More Religion

THE *Act of Uniformity* (1559) provides punishments and fines to be levied for various offenses against the established church.

Fine for failing to attend English prayer book services:
    Before 1580: 12d per guilty verdict
    After 1580:   £20 per month

Also after 1580, it is treason for you to convert to Catholicism or attempt to convert anyone else. Also to *reconcile* (reconvert) any English subject to Rome. The penalty is the same as for any other high treason: you will be hanged, drawn, and quartered, unless you are noble enough, in which case they'll cut off your head.

At any time, you can be fined and jailed for attending Mass or hiding a priest. More often prosecuted after 1580.

There are not very many (openly) Catholic priests left, anyway, since most of them converted along with the populace, accommodating to the prevailing wind. Said the vicar of Bray, having seen too many people burnt for their beliefs: "I always keep my principle, which is this—to live and die the Vicar of Bray."

There is an English college at Douai in France established specifically for training Catholic priests to return to England. At the end of the 1570s, these priests begin doing so and creating trouble. Edmund Campion is one of them.

The Catholic stronghold in England is in the North (notably Northumberland and Cumberland, but anything north of Norfolk). The Puritan stronghold is in the West Country (Devon, Somerset, and Cornwall.)

Of the two great universities, Oxford is said to be the most Catholic, Cambridge the "hot-bed of Lutherism".

Burghley, Bedford, and most of the other notable protestants were educated at Cambridge. However, Bedford sent his sons to Oxford.

Anyone may be required to swear to the *Oath of Supremacy*, which states that you believe that the Pope, being a foreign potentate, has not and ought not to have any spiritual power in

England. Peers are assumed to agree. Others may have to prove it.

> I, A. B., do utterly testify and declare in my conscience that the Queen's Highness is the only supreme governor of this realm, and of all other her Highness's dominions and countries, as well in all spiritual or ecclesiastical things or causes, as temporal, and that no foreign prince, person, prelate, state or potentate hath or ought to have any jurisdiction, power, superiority, pre-eminence or authority ecclesiastical or spiritual within this realm; and therefore I do utterly renounce and forsake all foreign jurisdictions, powers, superiorities and authorities, and do promise that from henceforth I shall bear faith and true allegiance to the Queen's Highness, her heirs and lawful successors, and to my power shall assist and defend all jurisdictions, pre-eminences, privileges and authorities granted or belonging to the Queen's Highness, her heirs or successors, or united or annexed to the imperial crown of this realm. So help me God, and by the contents of this Book.

The text of the Oath of Supremacy, 1559

People take an oath very seriously, and thus honest people are not inclined to swear to an oath they don't believe in.

Catholics find the oath troublesome because it requires them to renounce their allegiance to the Pope.

A redaction of salient points:

Montague boldly pointed out that the prince or commonwealth that will make a new law ought to consider three things: First, that it be necessary, then that it be just and reasonable, and finally that it be apt and fit to be put into execution. He argued:

Anthony Viscount Montague speaking in Parliament against the Oath of Supremacy, 1559

> For the first point, the law is not necessary because "the Catholics of this realm disturb not, nor hinder public affairs of the realm, neither spiritual nor temporal."

For the second point, it is neither just nor reasonable, for it is "contrary and repugnant to all laws of man, natural and civil. No man ought to be constrained in a matter he holds doubtful."

And for the third, the law is not enforceable. "What man is there without so much courage and stomach, or void of all honour that can consent... to receive an opinion and new religion by force and compulsion? ... And it is to be feared [that] rather than to die, they will seek out how to defend themselves."

As for the lay Lords, he added:

"Let them take good heed and not suffer themselves to be led by such men that are full of affection and passions, and that look to wax mighty and of power by the confiscation, spoil, and ruin of the houses of noble and ancient men."

Ranks & Files

THE ordinary ranking of the English Court, disregarding various offices, parents, patents, or orders of knighthood is as follows:

Men	Women
Duke	Duchess
Marquis (mar'-kwis)	Marchioness (mar'-shon-ess)
Earl	Countess
Viscount (vy'-count)	Viscountess (vy'-count-ess)
Baron	Baroness
Knight	Knight's lady

Royalty refers only to the monarch and his or her immediate family.

The Queen in Parliament

Nobility refers to peers and their families. The *peers* are barons and above, and sit by right in the House of Lords.

Gentry refers to anyone gentle but untitled, usually descended from nobility.

Knights are not noble. They are knightly. Knights and peers' sons may sit, by election or appointment, in the House of Commons.

An ordinary, undifferentiated knight is a *knight bachelor.*

Knight banneret is an honour conferred on a man who distinguishes himself on the battlefield in front of his monarch. It is a battlefield promotion which permits him to cut the tails off his pennon (making it a banner) and permits/requires him to lead a company of his own men under it. In Elizabeth's reign, there are only three, including Sir Ralph Sadler.

Sir Christopher Hatton

NOTE: *The rank of Baronet (a hereditary knighthood) will not exist until James I invents it as a money making scheme.*

Knights of the Garter outrank all the other knights.

In 1558, there were no more than about 600 knights in the country.

Minors and women holding rank in their own right may not sit in the House of Lords. Minors must wait till they are old enough. A woman may send her eldest son "in her right," when he comes of age.

Bishops and archbishops are ranked with the peers.

Bishops have a rank equal to that of an earl. *Archbishops* rank with the dukes. The Queen has little use for churchmen, however, and seldom invites them round to dine.

Precedence, Preferment & Attainder

P RECEDENCE refers to your rank, either above or below (or before or after) other people. An earl takes precedence over a baron, a baron over a knight, and so on. That is to say, he goes into dinner first, or gets his head cut off first; whatever.

Unmarried women take precedence from their fathers; married women from their husbands, with some exceptions.

A widowed countess who marries a mere knight is permitted in courtesy to retain the title and rank of a countess, though her husband does not become an earl, unless by royal grant.

An earl's daughter who marries a mere gentleman (as if!) would still be Lady *firstname*.

Strictly, precedence depends on birth (or marriage) and office, not on wealth, land, or popularity with the Queen.

For those of equal rank, precedence depends on the date of creation, not whether you are the 7th or 17th earl.

Date of creation is the year in which that title came to the family. The 3rd Earl of Derby (1485) outranks the 3rd Earl of Sussex (1529) who outranks the 3rd Earl of Southampton (1547).

The counting starts over if the title goes to a new family: William FitzWilliam, 1st Earl of Southampton was succeeded by Thomas Wriothesley, 1st Earl of Southampton, just to be confusing.

NOTE: Do not refer to *Titled Elizabethans* about this, as it continues the numbers from the beginning of time.

Precedence is affected by the government or royal household offices you may hold. Sir Christopher Hatton is "only" a knight, but when he is Lord Chancellor of England, he takes his precedence from that.

Maid of honour is a household office, and confers precedence, but not a title. A maid of honour takes precedence over a knight's lady, but *not* over an earl's daughter.

Preferment refers to offices, grants, monopolies, gifts, and other "perks" of court life. A major reason people go to Court is to gain preferment (or *advancement*).

Preferment does not necessarily imply a gain in precedence, just income.

A loss of preferment does not imply a loss of precedence, unless you lose an office that conferred some. An earl is still an earl, unless he's attainted.

The Queen has titles to bestow but does so very seldom. She created only a few new peers and as few knights as she could get away with.

Attainder refers to a person or family losing a noble title, plus any or all the rights and privileges attached to it, due to treason. The Crown may by a bill (or writ) of attainder deprive you and your family of lands and goods as well as your precedence and title, and possibly your life.

When Henry Wriothesley was attainted and in the Tower after the Essex Rebellion (1601) he was referred to as the "late Earl of Southampton".

Many great families have been attainted once or twice, including the Dudleys, Greys, and numerous Howards. It is not true that the Howards are born with a dotted line on their necks bearing the motto 𝕮𝖚𝖙𝖙𝖊 𝕳𝖊𝖗𝖊.

Queen Mary caused the Dudleys to be "restored in blood" so the remaining sons (Ambrose and Robert) could take their precedence as sons of a duke.

Queen Elizabeth made each of the Dudley boys an earl in his own right later on, although she restored Ambrose to his father's precedence as Earl of Warwick, which rather elevated him above his younger brother, Robert Earl of Leicester.

The Senior Peers of England

T HIS is just a very simple table, and it doesn't include the barons or bishops.

The creation date shown is when this branch of the family came into the senior title. For example, 1550 is the year John Russell was created Earl of Bedford.

Notice that Northampton has to die (without heirs) in 1572 before Viscount Hereford can become the Earl of Essex.

Viscounts do not have secondary titles. Modernly, an earl's second title is a viscounty. In period it is almost always a barony.

Title	Created	Surname	Secondary Title*
Dukes			
Norfolk	1483	Howard	E. Surrey
Marquises			
Northampton	1547	Parr	E. Essex
Winchester	1551	Paulet	E. Wiltshire, B. St. John
Earls			
Arundel	1137	Fitzalan	Maltravers
Oxford	1142	deVere	Vere
Northumber-land	1377	Percy	Percy
Westmoreland	1397	Neville	Neville of Raby
Shrewsbury	1442	Talbot	Furnival
Kent	1465	Grey de Ruthen	Grey
Derby	1485	Stanley	Strange
Worcester	1514	Somerset	Somerset
Rutland	1525	Manners	Roos
Cumberland	1525	Clifford	Clifford
Sussex	1529	Radcliffe	V. Fitzwalter, B. Fitzwalter
Huntington	1529	Hastings	Hastings
Bath	1536	Bourchier	Fitzwarrin
Warwick	1547	Dudley	Lisle
Southampton	1547	Wriothesley	Wriothesley of Titchfield
Bedford	1550	Russell	Russell of Cheynies

Title	Created	Surname	Secondary Title*
Earls (continued)			
Pembroke	1558	Herbert	Herbert
Hertford	1558	Seymour	Beauchamp
Leicester	1564	Dudley	Denbigh
Essex	1572	Devereaux	V. Hereford, B. Ferrers
Lincoln	1572	Fiennes	Clinton and Saye
Nottingham	1597	Howard	Howard of Effingham
Viscounts			
Montague	1554	Browne	
Bindon	1559	Howard	

* Codes: E. = Earl; B. = Baron; V. = Viscount

The Noble Style

THE prime proof of rank and nobility is liberality. People want to be known for their hospitality. The ideal is a substantial house, plenty of servants, and a lavish table where anyone is welcome.

As further evidence of liberality, the *broken meats* (table leavings) are customarily given to the poor at the kitchen door. For Catholics, this also counts as "good works".

As a great compliment, it was said of the 3rd Earl of Derby: "His house in plenty was ever maintained."

This has to be tempered by the need to live within one's income and avoid oppressing the tenantry to raise the cash. One Earl and Countess of Rutland got so carried away that

Giving alms to a beggar

the Crown intervened, in the interest of preserving the ancient honours, and put them on a budget of £200 a year!

Income is usually discussed as rentals, and does not take into account profits from offices, industry, land farmed by the lord himself, profits of court, bribes, douceurs, and sale of offices.

Very few noblemen have an accurate notion of their full income, gross or net. That's what you have servants for.

Sources   Stone: *Crisis of the Aristocracy*
           Stone: *Family & Fortune*

Honour & Dueling

...is nowhere described better than by Lawrence Stone in *Crisis of the Aristocracy*:

> Tempers were short and weapons easy to hand. The basic characterics of the nobility, like those of the poor, were ferocity and childishness and lack of self control.

Calling someone a liar, or otherwise impugning his honour, his courage, or his name is a challenge in itself.

Dueling is illegal, so you take the fight out of the way, and sometimes out of the country (any war zone will do). Usually this is single combat, unlike the group duels of France, which lead to longstanding feuds.

If you are angry enough, you may not wait for a duel, or even for a fair fight. One (or some) of your men may lie in ambush. People get killed this way all the time, though often it's a gentleman's retainers who take the brunt of the attack.

Sir John Hawkins was killed by someone who mistook him for Sir Christopher Hatton. Sir Drew Drury was killed in a dispute over precedence.

Stone: *Crisis of the Aristocracy*   *Sources*
Dr Ron Love, workshop discussions, 1980–83

The City of London

FROM the report of a Venetian envoy, about 1500:

> It abounds with every article of luxury, as well as with the necessities of life. But the most remarkable thing in London is the wonderful quantity of wrought silver. I do not allude

to that in private houses, but to the shops of London. In one single street, named the Strand, leading to St Paul's, there are fifty-two goldsmith's shops, so rich and full of silver vessels, great and small, that in all the shops in Milan, Rome, Venice, and Florence put together, I do not think there would be found so many of the magnificence that are to be seen in London. And these vessels are all either salt cellars or drinking cups or basins to hold water for the hands, for they eat off that fine tin [pewter] which is a little inferior to silver.

These great riches of London are not occasioned by its inhabitants being noblemen or gentlemen; being all, on the contrary, persons of low degree, and artificers who have congregated there from all parts of the island, and from Flanders and from every other place.

The English are great lovers of themselves, and of everything belonging to them. They think that there are no other men than themselves, and no other world but England. And whenever they see a handsome foreigner, they say that he looks like an Englishman, and that it is a great pity that he should not be an Englishman. And when they partake of any delicacy with a foreigner, they ask him whether such a thing is made in their country. They take great pleasure in having a quantity of excellent victuals, and also in remaining a long time at table, being very sparing of wine when they drink it at their own expense.

From *Shakespeare*, by Anthony Burgess, 1978:

> Ale was the standard tipple, and it was strong. Ale for breakfast
> was a good means of starting the day in euphoria or truculence.
> Ale for dinner refocillated the wasted tissues of the morning.
> Ale for supper ensured a heavy snoring repose. The better sort
> drank wine, which promoted good fellowship and led to sword
> fights. It was not what we would call a sober city.

More Comparative Religion: Calvinists

CALVINISTS include Puritans, Huguenots, Presbyterians, etc. For their particular twist on things, refer to the Anglicans, then stir in the following.

God already knows who is to be saved or damned. No action on any one's part can change this *predestination*. The limited number of those already saved are called the *Elect*.

Good works are expected of the Elect, but are not required for salvation. They are not Saved because they are virtuous; they are virtuous because they are Saved.

The *prayers* of priests are no more perfect, and no more important to God, than others.

Testifying, or preaching and interpreting Scripture, is encouraged and expected of both ministers and the congregation.

The prayers of noblemen are no more valuable to God, either. Every man is equal in the sight of God. This is dangerously revolutionary thinking.

The rituals of the English church are still too Roman to suit the Puritans. They would prefer that candles, bells, saints and vestments of any kind be removed.

Certain evangelical preachers are even more radical. They also maintain that Scripture is not the only source of God's truth because it is still possible for the Holy Spirit to speak through an individual. A man (or more rarely, a woman) can have personal revelations not only of the nature of God but about matters of daily life.

While revelation is an intensely personal experience, the person so visited has an obligation to communicate his vision with the rest of the Christian community.

Still More Language: Alternatives

Instead of...	Say...
Okay	Very well
	'Tis done
	As you will
	Marry shall I
	Aye, and with a good will
Wow!	Marry!
	I' faith!
	Hey-ho!
	God's Death! (or teeth or any other body part)
	What ho!
	'Zounds (God's wounds, pron: *zoonds*)
Excuse me	Forgive me
	Pray pardon
	I crave your forgiveness
	By your leave

Instead of…	Say…
Darn it!	Fie! Fie on't Fie on thee (but *not* "fie me") By Cock, by God, by heaven, etc.
Please	Prithee (I pray thee) If you please An thou likest An it please you By your leave An thou wilt An you will
Thank you	Gramercy I thank thee My thanks God reward thee
Gesundheit!	God save you!
Air head	Light-minded Airling
Bottom line	In the end At bottom In the main Finally At the last
Bathroom	Privy Jakes Ajax Little room of office

Instead of...	Say...
Certainly!	Surely
	Aye marry
	Assuredly
	Certes (sir'-tees)
	USAGE NOTE: Certes means certainly, not certain. Do not say "I am certes that I paid that account." And never use it to replace "sure" as in: "For certes, they will soon be married."
Hello	Good day, good morrow, good e'en
	God ye good'en (or just good'en)
	God save you, sweet mistress
	How now, Sir Toby Belch
Nay not	Nay, I shall not
	Nay, it is not so
	(Just say "nay")

Household Management

R ENTS are due and servants are paid on the traditional
quarter days, so called because they divide the year into
quarters. Curiously, each of these falls on or about an equinox
or solstice.

USAGE NOTE: This is quarter day, *not* quartering day!

Quarter Day	Date	What it's about
Lady Day	March 25	Feast of the Annunciation. When the Angel Gabriel told Mary she would be the mother of Christ. Also, since 1155 (and until 1752), the first day of the new year in the legal calendar, even though New Year's is still celebrated in January.
Midsummer Day	June 24	Feast of St. John the Baptist. It is midsummer because summer, as humans perceive it in Northern Europe, begins on May Day.
Michaelmas	September 29	Feast of St. Michael the Archangel. Celebrations in the North often include horses: racing, selling, stealing, etc. And something to do with carrots.
Christmas Day	December 25	The birth of Christ. A feast day but less important than Easter.

A note on the new year

You may pay for some services *in kind* instead of money: such as an amount of firewood, the use of land, or a number of fish from your stream by the quarter or by the year.

In the country . . .

Some tenants may pay part of their rents in kind: calves, honey, milk, wool, etc.

The lady of the house, even a noble lady, may do or at least oversee many homely things herself, such as the brewing of ale or mead. Even noble ladies take responsibility for making shirts for the gentlemen of the house.

If you live mostly in the country, you are likely to be very proud of your ale, or how pure your milk is, or what excellent honey your bees produce.

Bees love gossip. It is considered lucky for your estate and family to tell the bees every bit of news. If you don't, they may leave and take their good luck with them.

Science & Health (without key to the scriptures)

E VERYTHING in the world is composed of four elements: *Earth, Air, Fire, and Water.*

In the human body, the humours are the natural bodily fluids. They correspond to the elements and have various qualities: cold, dry, hot, and moist.

The nature or *complexion* of anything is a combination of two of these humourous qualities.

Here is a simple chart of the relationships of the humours and elements. Most people are aware of this chart to some degree. (Hypochondriacs have it memorized.)

Element	Humour	Quality	Nature
Fire	Choler (yellow bile)	Hot and dry	Choleric (angry, temperamental)
Air	Blood	Hot and moist	Sanguine (jolly, lusty)
Water	Phlegm	Cold and moist	Phlegmatic (sluggish, slow)
Earth	Melancholy (black bile)	Cold and dry	Melancholic (sad, lovesick)

When the humours are all in balance in a person, he or she is completely healthy. If they get out of balance, illness results. Doctors *bleed* their patients to restore this balance, because blood is considered to have preeminence over the other humours.

Bleeding is performed with a *fleam* (lancet) and a bowl, not with leeches (ick). In fact, leeching is a separate type of operation.

Blood is usually drawn from the arm or the foot. Someone with a natural abundance of choler is said to be *choleric*, or naturally angry and quick-tempered. (Does that mean you could call them 'pissy'?)

Black bile is considered to be the foam off the top of the blood. Whatever that is.

Andrew Boorde's *Breviary of Health* is a popular text around many households for advice on staying healthy.

The *liver*, not the heart, is considered the source of the emotions, although the heart is the source of love. The *stomach* is the seat of courage. The *spleen* is the source of anger.

> There is nothing that doth comfort the heart so much beside God as honest mirth and good company. And wine moderately taken doth comfort the heart, and good bread doth confirm and steady a man's heart. And all good and temperate drinks the which doth engender good blood doth comfort the heart. All manner of cordials and restoratives and all sweet and soothing things do comfort the heart, and so doth nutmeg and ginger and poached eggs not hard, their yolks a cordial... But above all things, mirth is best to bedward.
> —Andrew Boorde, *A Breviary of Health*, 1547

Ireland

WHAT *does an ordinary Englishman know (or think he knows) about Ireland? Simple beliefs (as opposed to simple facts) are marked with* :~.

:~ The weather is dreadful, the morals of the people worse. They need to be dragged kicking and screaming into the civilized 16th century, or be eliminated.

On the other hand, the girls are pretty, buxom, and willing.

:~ It's nothing but bogs and marshes and Catholics who speak no English or other human tongue.

On the other hand, there's land for the taking for any gentleman adventurer with the guts to go get it and hang onto it.

:~ The country is a dagger aimed at England, for use by Spain or any other Catholic power, and thus must be subdued and made as English as possible.

The English Crown never seems to provide enough money, men, or supplies. Ireland just sucks up whatever we send over there, and nothing ever seems to be accomplished.

There has been an English presence in Ireland since 1172, when an Irish king invited English knights in to take care of some earlier invaders.

English government is centered in Dublin and the area around it, called The Pale.

Lord Sussex, Sir Henry Sidney, Sir William FitzWilliam, Lord Grey, and others have taken a shot at governing it with varying degrees of success.

Shane O'Neill and (later) his nephew Hugh O'Neill give us the most trouble in the northern parts of Ireland. The English title they hold is Earl of Tyrone.

Gerald Fitzgerald Earl of Desmond, with his cousins, gives us the most trouble in the southern parts.

The earls of Ormond and Kildare are our allies; Kildare's mother was English, and he is married to Lady Southampton's sister Mabel.

The English in general behave very badly while on duty in Ireland, even gentlemen of otherwise pleasant disposition. Must be the rain.

Sources   Berleth: *The Twilight Lords*
Morrison: *Itineraries*
Derrick: *An Image of Irland*

Ireland in the 1500s

Scotland

WHAT *does an ordinary Englishman know (or think he knows) about Scotland? Simple beliefs (as opposed to simple facts) are marked with ∶∼.*

The capital of the country is Edinburgh (ed'-in-buh-ruh); we've almost captured it once or twice.

∶∼ It is overrun with Frenchmen, which means it is a continuing threat on our northern flank and ought to be subdued by England for our own good. (In fact, the "Auld Alliance" with France is dead by 1570.)

∶∼ The Scots are untrustworthy, incapable of keeping a bargain, a treaty, or their word, even amongst themselves. There is no word for *loyalty* in Scottish.

∶∼ Barely civilized, they are almost as bad as the Irish.

The Borders comprise the West, Middle and East Marches of England, facing the West, Middle, and East Marches of Scotland. Each march is governed by a warden.

Being *at feud* is a way of life. A truce may be pledged and may include marriages between feuding families, although this does not create a permanent peace.

A common soldier in the border garrison at Berwick (bear'-ick) gets food, clothing, equipment, and earns 8 pence a day, from which 4 pence is kept back for food, clothing, equipment.

Although still in transition, Scotland is rapidly going protestant. Scottish protestants are Presbyterians, following the Calvinist teachings of John Knox. The Highlands are predominantly Catholic.

In the Lowlands, the proper term is "family", not "clan". Clan is a Gaelic word.

The word Celt is not used in English until the early 18th century. Various clansmen should be referred to as Irish or Scots, or even "Scotch", which is the period word for Scottish.

The clans are tribal Highlanders of the far north, who do not speak English. The fighting on the borders never involves Highland troops.

The English have a stake in keeping the situation on the border unstable. As long as the Scots government has to spend time and money trying to maintain the peace at home, it's not making war on England.

Sources   Fraser: *The Steel Bonnets*
           Fraser: *Mary Queen of Scots*

Mary Queen of Scots (1542–1587)
an incredibly brief account

SHE is Mary Stuart (originally *Stewart*), daughter of James V of Scotland and Marie de Guise, daughter of the duke of Lorraine. She was Queen of Scots from the time she was six days old. She was a staunch Catholic until she died.

She is not "Bloody Mary." That charming title belongs to Elizabeth's sister, Mary Tudor, who created a lot of *protestant* martyrs.

Mary Stuart's grandmother was Henry VIII's sister Margaret. Henry's will and the Act of Succession excluded this branch from the English succession, but since Elizabeth is officially a bastard and heretic (according to the Pope), Mary believes she

Mary Queen of Scots

is the rightful Queen of England. A lot of people (mainly foreigners and English Catholics) agree with her.

She became Queen of France and Scotland by marrying the French prince who became Francis II, who died in 1560. Widowed at the age of 18 she returned to Scotland the following year.

In 1565 she married Henry Stuart Lord Darnley, son of the countess of Lennox, a granddaughter of Henry VII. Their son James was born in July 1566. Her husband, who had all the morals of an ape, was a jerk and conspired against her.

While Darnley was convalescing in '68 (of a "shameful illness") he was killed when the basement of the house he was staying in exploded. However, he was not killed in the explosion. His body was found in the garden, stabbed and strangled. Many people accused Mary of arranging it.

In May of 1568, after a variety of military actions and her third marriage (to the earl of Bothwell, possibly by force) she left Scotland to throw herself on England's mercy. Various Stuart, Tudor, and deGuise ancestors proceeded to roll over in their graves.

She spent 19 years in England, with various jailers at various houses. Elizabeth wouldn't agree to see her until Mary had been cleared of the accusation of murdering her husband, but Mary claimed (rightfully) that a foreign court had no right to try her, a sovereign queen. Several investigations produced a number of damning letters, possibly forged, but nothing was ever resolved.

In captivity, she eventually signed papers officially abdicating in favor of her son. During this time, her special emissaries to Elizabeth were Sir James Melville and John Leslie, Bishop of Ross.

A number of serious plots revolved around her, the main ones being the Ridolfi Plot (to marry her to Norfolk and place them both on the English throne, with Spanish help) and the Babington Plot (to kill Elizabeth, rescue Mary, and put her on the throne, possibly with French help). The latter plot is covered nicely in part 5 of the BBC's *Elizabeth R*.

In 1586, Mary was tried in England by a panel of peers and justices, and condemned. Elizabeth put off signing the death warrant as long as she could, but Mary was executed at last on 7 February 1587, at Fotheringhay Castle.

Sources   Dunn: *Elizabeth and Mary—Cousins, Rivals, Queens*
Fraser: *Mary Queen of Scots*
Gristwood: *Elizabeth & Leicester*

Shopping in London

Y ou do not "go shopping". You go to the shops or you go
to market.

The Royal Exchange in London, built by Sir Thomas Gresham, was opened by the Queen in 1571, just in time for the
shopping season, as sort of an Elizabethan shopping mall. A
very prestigious building in the classical style, fine merchants
of all sorts have set up shop here.

The main building features a huge, gilded grasshopper on
the roof: Gresham's personal badge.

One-stop-shopping includes: Feather shops, Milliners, Wig
makers, Ready made clothes (drapers), Imported accessories,
Embroidered goods, Perfumes, Starches (used for ruffs).

From John Stowe, *A Survey of London*, 1603:

Trade	Street, Neighborhood, or District
Mercers and haberdashers	West Cheape & London Bridge
Goldsmiths	Gutherons Lane
Pepperers and grocers	Bucklesberrie
Drapers	Lombard Street and Cornhill
Skinners	St. Mary Pellipers, Budge Row & Walbrooke
Stock-fishmongers	Thames Street
Wet-fishmongers	Knight-riders Street & Bridge Street
Ironmongers	Ironmongers Lane, Old Jurie & Thames Street
Vintners	The Vintree and various corners
Wigmakers	Silver Street
Brewers	Near the river (it's the water!)

When you can't find it at the Exchange…

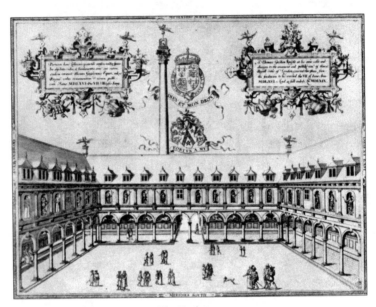

The Exchange

The most exclusive jewelers and mercers are in Cheapside.

You can buy second-hand clothes in Birchin Lane, but people "of appearance" do not shop there.

There are no zoning laws. Shops, taverns, and residences live noisily side by side all over the city.

Most of the really low company you may be looking for is probably hanging out in Southwark across the river. (Pronounce it suth'-ook: "th" as in "bathe" and "ook" as in "hook".)

Naturally the bear garden (for bear baiting) is here, as are, eventually, the play houses and many of the stews.

Sources   Burgess: Shakespeare
Stowe: *A Survey of London*, 1603
Williams: *All the Queen's Men*

A Fashionable Vocabulary: Clothing & Fabrics

Thus it is now come to pass, that women are become men, and men transformed into monsters.
—Wm Harrison, *A Description of England*, 1577

THE jeweled roll at the front of your French hood is called a *billiment*.

A necklace is commonly called a *carcanet* (kar'-ka-net) before about 1575, when the word necklace comes into use.

Gardes or *welts* are ornamental bands, often edging a gown or forepart, but also used as strips of trim.

Lace is a general term for all kinds of trims and braids, as well as cords or points to fasten a garment.

Lucerne is lynx fur. Other furs are marten, sable, and so on.

Needle lace

Cloth of gold is gold metal thread woven on a linen or silk warp, and may come in colors, especially crimson or violet, depending on the color of the warp thread.

Pinks and *cuttes* are small, decorative cuts on the fabric. *Slashes* are larger, and may have the lining pulled through.

When a fabric is described as *printed*, the design has been stamped with hot irons.

The lightweight silk you lined your slashes with is probably *sarcenet* (sar'-sa-net); so called because it was understood to have originated with the Saracens.

Your gold trim is really *silver-gilt* thread or *Venice gold*. Your good glass pearls are *Venice* or *Venetian pearls*. (You wouldn't wear the natural ones on Progress, now would you? Of course not.)

You might tell an interested party that your very fine, sheer, cotton shift or partlet is made of *lawn* (very fine linen). Those of China silk (habotai) are probably of *cypress*.

What we call changeable taffeta can also be called *shot silk*. What they called taffeta was a much different fabric.

Merchant class women (citizens' or burgesses' wives) do not always wear a *bumroll* and seldom wear a *farthingale*. See drawings by Lucas de Heere and the "Wedding at Bermondsey" painting for examples.

All kinds of pants (*slops* or *venetians*, etc.) are called *hose*, specifically trunk hose, because they cover the trunk of the body.

Another, less vulgar, term for slops is *round paned hose*.

Hose that cover the lower part of the leg are called *nether hose* or nether stocks.

We go brave in our apparel that we may be taken for better men than we be. We use much bombastings and quiltings to seem fitter formed, better shouldered, smaller waisted, fuller

thighed than we are. We barbe and shave often to seem younger than we are. We use perfumes both inward and outward
to seem sweeter than we be. We use courteous salutations to
seem kinder than we are; and sometimes graver and Godlier
communications to seem wiser than we be.

—Sir John Harrington

Forms of Address for Common Folk

T HE term *gentles* should be reserved for those who are of *Gentry*
gentle birth: noblemen, knights, and their descendants
(with or without titles). To address a crowd, say "good folk" or
"good people" or some such thing; not "good gentles".

The gentry are un-titled landholders, who come from noble families. In particular, they are descendents of younger sons of the nobility.

Gentility has to do with land-owning and ancestry, not good manners, though manners may be considered a mark of gentility.

Only those of gentle birth are addressed as Master and Mistress.

Gentle birth also has little to do with money. You may be gentle and "land poor", meaning you have plenty of land but no cash. This sometimes applies to noble families, though it is not fair to say that any merchant has more money than any nobleman.

Knightly class Knights are not noble but they are gentry. Knighthood is not hereditary.

A knighthood is essentially a battlefield honour, sometimes given for other kinds of service. Walsingham's is for diplomacy, you might say.

Knighthood no longer comes with land or an income, as it did in earlier times, although it will require you to spend more to maintain your estate or standing.

Sir Henry Sidney turned down a barony because he believed he couldn't afford to maintain a baron's estate.

The middling sort The term *middle class* is unknown in period. People are much more specific about their place in society. Say instead: merchants, yeoman, burgesses, citizens, and so on.

The *yeomanry* are essentially prosperous, non-gentle (and non-husbandmen) tenants, worth no less than £6 per annum, according to Harrison. Their landlords are the gentlemen landowners.

When yeomen get a little money, they tend to buy land, which makes them landowners, but still not gentry. Address them as Goodman and Goodwife, but not Master or Mistress.

If the family is provident and continues to acquire and hold the land for at least three generations, they can apply to be counted among the gentry.

Citizens and burgesses may be considered the urban equivalent to the yeoman class.

Refer to this solid backbone of England as good folk or sturdy yeomen.

In the countryside, the lowest rung on the social ladder are those tenants (*cottars* or *husbandmen*, but rarely *peasants*) who work on someone else's land for wages. They pay rent in money but also in kind and in services. They are often in debt. Their employers are often yeoman farmers. *Working men*

In town, people who do common labor for wages are simply *laborers*. Harrison (1577) lists tailors, shoemakers, carpenters, brickmakers, masons, and other *handicraftmen* as having the same social standing.

City people of any rank consider themselves superior to country people of the same sort.

Think of them as common, rustic, or lesser folk or villagers, husbandmen, or something else pleasant but non-gentle. In Shakespeare, "peasant" is used only as a term of abuse. He preferred to call them handicraftmen and "rude mechanicals."

Your liveried *retainers* are not peasants (even if their parents are).

Some sources   Harrison: *Description of England*
Smith: *De republica anglorum*, 1583

What We Eat

ELIZABETHAN cookery is generally sweeter than today's; meats are often cooked with fruits, producing a mix of sweet and savory.

Some medical texts advise against eating raw vegetables as engendering wind (gas) or evil humours.

It is important to remember that while many things were period somewhere, not everything was eaten in every part of the world. Things which are common in Constantinople may never make their way to England.

The *potato* is still a novelty. It is not yet a crop in Ireland, nor is it found in our stews. The turnip, which has that honour, is followed closely by the parsnip.

Tomatoes are considered doubtful, if not actually poisonous, although they have begun to appear in some southern European cooking.

Chocolate has not yet come in, except for medicinal purposes. *Flavours*
The Swiss have not yet added milk and sugar to it. If you have
ever tasted chocolate (which is very doubtful) it was a thin and
bitter drink, and probably flavored with chilies.

The much-touted St. John's Bread (carob) may taste somewhat like chocolate but it is not being used as a flavoring in
sweets.

Just to be fair, vanilla isn't a period flavoring in Europe
either.

Almond is the most common flavoring in sweets, followed by
cinnamon, clove, and saunders (sandalwood).

Almond milk, ground almonds steeped in honey and water or
wine, then strained, is used as flavoring and thickener.

Coffee is period in the strictest sense, but has not arrived in
England.

The law says we may not eat meat on Fridays and Saturdays. *Fish days*
This is not a religious fast but a way of supporting the fishing
industry. Exceptions are made by special license for the old, the
very young, and the infirm, and anyone else who applies for the
license.

A typical fish day meal can include eggs, butter, cheese, her-
ring, cod or other whitefish, etc.

Sugar is available, but is rather more expensive than honey, *Sugar*
since it has to be imported. Grown as sugar cane, it comes as a
3- or 4-pound square or conical loaf, and has to be grated or
pounded into useful form.

The finest sugar (from Madera) is white and melts easily in
liquid.

The next grade is Barbary or Canary sugar.

The common, coarse sugar is brown and rather gluey, good
for syrups and seasoning meat.

Spain, France, Germany, Italy
& other despicable places

THE English are professionally paranoid of anything foreign. The word *insular* might have been coined to describe us.

On the other hand, we are habitually envious of all things foreign: Italian manners, French fashions, Spanish gold, etc.

We have always been enemies with the French, except when necessary to unite against Spain.

On the other hand, we have often been allied with Spain, until that unfortunate episode of the Armada in 1588.

Spain In her will, Mary Queen of Scots left her claim to England to King Philip of Spain, which provided him with the impetus to finally launch the Enterprise of England.

Philip's primary motive was both religious (really wanting to bring England back to the Roman Catholic church) and political (wanting to keep France surrounded.)

France At the time of Richard the Lionheart (1188–1199) the Plantagenet empire included England, Normandy, Anjou, Aquitaine, and vast tracts of France. Also the lordship of Ireland.

By the time of Bloody Mary (1553–1558), the only English possession on the Continent was the town of Calais, opposite Dover, on the French coast.

We lost Calais (pronounced cal'-iss by the English) in a war with the French about 1556–57. The English were severely depressed over this loss. Queen Mary said that when she died, they would open her up and find the word Calais written over her heart.

Like Spain, France is a Roman Catholic country. French *protestant*s are Calvinists called Huguenots (pronounced hew'-ga-nots by Englishmen).

In the St. Bartholomew's Day Massacre, 1572, the king allowed thousands of Huguenots to be massacred in religious riots throughout the country. Even English Catholics were shocked and appalled.

The French Calvinists have asked the English, as co-religionists, for money and military aid. They will not get it till 1625.

Germany is not a country but a collection of little "countries", *Germany* whose people all speak some dialect more or less recognizable as German. We English refer to it as "the Germanies".

The *Empire* refers to the Holy Roman Empire: in the middle of the century, it includes most of the German states, Spain, Flanders, and even parts of Italy. Border disputes with France are common. There has also been a good deal of fighting in Italy.

The Empire, particularly Spain, claims the Netherlands and keeps trying to establish sovereignty there.

The Dutch have also asked for English men, money, arms, and officers. When we say we are fighting in the Low Countries, this is where we mean.

The Landsknechts are crack mercenary troops from all over the Empire, primarily from the German states. In the Continental wars, Germans tend to be employed by the English, Swiss by the French.

Their life is so nasty, brutish, and short that the Emperor Maximilian granted them dispensation from all sumptuary laws, which explains their flamboyant attire. ("Max said we could!" is a period expression.)

Germans come in both Catholic and protestant varieties. It is safe to say that most German protestants are Lutherans. Swiss protestants tend to be Calvinists.

Both the Catholics and the Lutherans despise the Calvinists as well as each other, and the Calvinists return the sentiment (one of the benefits of revealed Truth). There is no conformity among protestant sects.

Italy Like Germany, Italy is not a country but a language group.

The Italian peninsula is made up of a number of city-states such as Florence, Genoa, Venice, Milan and so on, ruled by powerful families such as the Medici, Gonzaga, Borgia, Sforza, and so on, respectively.

As well as being the center of the Catholic Church, Rome is the center of the secular political territory called the Papal States, ruled by the Pope.

Since the Pope is a temporal ruler as well as a spiritual one, it is possible to declare war on him, which Catholic rulers (such as King Philip) have done.

Italians and Spaniards are most likely to be Catholic, although there are feeble protestant movements in both places, effectively countered by the Inquisition.

Children & Childhood

A little boy is dressed in skirts, pretty much like his sister. When he is between 3 and 7, depending on his parents' and nurse's assessment, he gets his first pair of *breeches* or breech hose.

This event, called *breeching*, is celebrated with a party. The boy is now said to have been breeched. Before this he was just "an unbreeched boy."

Infants are wrapped in *swaddling bands* for the first 6 to 12 months. It is considered unhealthy to give them the free use of their limbs.

Bastards cannot legally own or inherit property, hold public or ecclesiastical office, marry, or any number of ordinary things. It is not a romantic thing to be. A bastard "deserves to be slapped."

Hugh Rhodes's *Book of Nurture* (1577) provides lessons in the behavior expected from children and, presumably, from properly brought up adults. After all, "If a youth be void of virtue, in age he shall lack honour."

Here are a few of them. I have [distilled] some longer ones to an easier mouthful.

- Reverence thy father and mother as Nature requires.
- [If you have been out of their presence for a long while, ask their blessing.]
- Stand not too fast in thy conceit.
- Rise early in the morning to be holy, healthy, and wealthy.
- [Say your morning prayers.]
- [In church, kneel, sit, or stand devoutly. Do not cast your eyes about or chatter with women, priests, or clerks.]
- At dinner, press not thyself too high; sit in the place appointed thee.
- Sup not loud of thy pottage.
- Dip not thy meat in the saltcellar, but take it with a knife.
- Belch near no man's face with a corrupt fumosity.
- Eat small morsels of meat; eat softly, and drink mannerly.
- Corrupt not thy lips with eating, as a pig doth.

- Scratch not thy head with thy fingers, nor spit you over the table.
- If your teeth be putrefied, it is not right to touch meat that others eat.
- Wipe thy mouth when thou shalt drink ale or wine on thy napkin only, not on the table cloth. Blow not your nose in the napkin where ye wipe your hand.
- [Chew with your mouth closed.]

Heirs & Inheritance

MALE *primogeniture* is the rule. That is, the eldest son inherits everything (including debts) unless provision is otherwise made for younger sons. In particular, he gets the title if there is one.

The Court of Wards

The eldest son gets the title and so on, even if the oldest child is a girl.

Very rarely, a title and lands may pass in the female line. For example, a secondary title to the Manners earls of Rutland is the barony of deRoos (one of the oldest in the kingdom), in which the title passes simply to the eldest child, regardless of gender. Although her younger cousin (as eldest male) became the earl, Lady Elizabeth Manners (as eldest child) became the Baroness de Roos in her own right.

A will also makes provision for a daughter's dowry, which the heir is bound to honour.

When a peer dies leaving a minor heir, that child becomes a ward of the Crown. That is, the Crown takes responsibility for the education and marriage of the heir until he comes of age at 21.

The costs of this responsibility are paid out of the third of the deceased peer's estate that is dedicated to the upbringing of the heir as a Crown ward. The office of Master of Wards (held for a long time by Burghley) is a very lucrative one. Other orphans are managed by the Court of Orphans.

Often some other gentleman applies to buy the marriage rights of such a ward, and takes the responsibility (and the income) for the child's upbringing. Usually this means taking the child into his own home, administering their estate, and profiting from the result.

Sometimes the heir's mother is awarded these rights herself.

When the heir comes of age, he must sue the crown for the return of his livery and maintenance.

An heiress is a daughter with no brothers and no clear male heirs. If there are several girls, they will be co-heiresses. This can get complex. Consult a herald.

When there are only daughters and no clear male heir, the property is divided among the girls, and the title goes into *abeyance* until or unless a male heir can be proved. Eventually it may be awarded to someone completely new.

A bastard is a child born out of wedlock. By law, any child born to a married woman is legitimate, with some exceptions. If you are living openly with another man and having his children, your lawful husband doesn't have to accept them as his own.

A bastard is also called a natural child. Illegitimate children can be *legitimated* only by royal decree.

The "bend sinister" across a coat of arms does *not* indicate bastardy. Bastards are not entitled to their fathers' coat of arms without special application, when any of several marks maybe used for this purpose.

Sources   Fox-Davies: *A Complete Guide to Heraldry*
Stone: *Family and Fortune*
Stone: *Crisis of the Aristocracy*
Williams: *All the Queen's Men*

Naming the Baby

ENGLISHMEN do not have middle names, as a rule. Middle names are in general found only in Europe, especially in Germany and Spain, until the 17th century. Where we find them in some lists, the odds are good that the records from which they were taken were contradictory, illegible, or wrong.

I can think of only three English exceptions; each is a curiosity and has a reason:

Jane Sybilla Morrison
Stepdaughter to the 2nd earl of Bedford, born abroad.

Thomas Posthumous Hoby
Son of Sir Thomas Hoby and Elizabeth Cook, born after his father's death (that is, posthumously).

Anthony Maria Browne
Lord Montague's grandson, 5th in an unbroken sequence of Anthony Brownes, and born in the lifetime of both his father and grandfather. Perhaps given in honour of his aunt, Mary, the countess of Southampton.

We do not put Junior after a name, or use "the Third" except when counting monarchs. We may, however, say "the Younger" to refer to the junior generation.

It is not true that there are only five names each for men and women in England; it just seems that way. The most common names for girls appear to be: Elizabeth, Anne/Agnes, Jane, Mary/Margaret, and Katherine. And for boys: Henry, Thomas, Edward, John, William, and Robert.

People sometimes use nicknames, but only with intimates, children, or servants. Some of these familiar names maybe unfamiliar to you:

Use...	For...	Use...	For...
Jack	John	Kit	Christopher
Nan	Anne	Meg	Margaret
Harry or Hal	Henry	Robin	Robert
Ned	Edward	Nell	Eleanor or Helen
Bess	Elizabeth	Kate or Kitty	Katherine
Mall or Molly	Mary	Jennet	Jane

Nominal curiosities Names like Lettyce (for Letitia), Douglas, Peregrine, Fulke, Susan, Valentine, Joyce, Reginald, and even Ambrose are more or less unique.

James is common only in Scotland until near the end of Elizabeth's reign.

Joan is a common or country form of *Jane*, rendered in Latin as Johanna.

Mary and *Margaret* appear to be more or less interchangeable in parish records.

Bridget is not particularly Irish, but is a fairly ordinary English girl's name.

Magdelyn is pronounced "Madelyn" or "Mawdlin". Agnes is pronounced and sometimes spelled Anys ("an'-nis".)

When a child dies, the next child may be given the same name.

Children are often named for a *godparent* whom the parents wish to honour. This is another reason why we often find duplicate names in the same generation.

Most given names come from relatives and godparents, rather than current trends.

Duffy: *Voices of Morepath*   *Sources*
Laning: *Faire Names for English Folk*
Jones: *The Birth of the Elizabethan Age*

The Queen's Suitors: The Short List

ARCHDUKE CHARLES VON HAPSBURG   *The foreign*
   The Emperor's second son. Negotiations on and off from   *contingent*
   1564–67. Supported by Cecil, undermined by Leicester who
   still has aspirations. Represented at court by his Chamberlain, vonBreumer.

FRANCOIS DE VALOIS, DUC D'ALENÇON ET D'ANJOU
   The younger brother to the king of France. Negotiations
   throughout the late '70s. His mother is Catherine di Medici.
   Fairly serious. Supported by Burghley, opposed by Walsingham and Hatton. Representation: Baron Jean de Simier.

ROBERT DUDLEY, EARL OF LEICESTER
   A widower after 1563, but perpetually under a cloud because
   of the manner of his wife Amy's death. With Cecil, HRM's
   best friend--except when he's being a jerk. Out of contention
   after '78 when he is married to Lettyce Knollys.

Robert Dudley, Earl of Leicester

KING ERIC OF SWEDEN

Not considered a good bet, although he sends lots of presents. Representation: his brother Duke John of Finland and sister Princess Cecilia with her husband the Margrave von Baden Baden. (GOSSIP: Cecilia was known to be "flirting heavily" with the Earl of Arundel in 1567.)

KING PHILIP OF SPAIN

Briefly imagines he has a chance, since he used to be married to her sister. The queen let him think so for a while at the beginning of the reign, then the matter was dropped.

EMANUEL PHILIBERT, DUKE OF SAVOY

Originally proposed by Philip of Spain when Elizabeth was still the Lady Elizabeth. Savoy has almost nothing to recommend him except a title and a swagger. Most of his duchy has been taken by the French, and he's broke. No threat, no advantage.

English hopefuls (besides Leicester) include at various times: *English hopefuls*

+ Sir Christopher Hatton
+ Sir William Pickering
+ Henry Fitzalan, earl of Arundel
+ Thomas Howard, duke of Norfolk
+ Sir Thomas Heneage

Williams: *All the Queen's Men* *Source*

The Royal Sweepstakes

ACCORDING to the will of Henry VIII, the legal heirs to his throne were his children: Edward, Mary, then Elizabeth. By the principle of male primogeniture, sons always come first, even when they are younger than their sisters.

King Henry VIII

After the King's children (should they all die childless), the order by custom should have been:

1. Margaret, Henry's elder sister, who married King James IV of Scotland and
   - Her children and their heirs, then
   - Her children by her second husband, the Earl of Angus, then
2. Mary, Henry's younger sister, who married (secondly) Charles Brandon, duke of Suffolk, then
   - Her children and their heirs.

However, for some reason, Henry disinherited his elder sister, so technically the Scottish claims are all bogus—according to the old king's will, which Parliament has confirmed as the *Act of Succession*.

Blood (and policy) is often more important than statute. Hence the real threat of the Stuart claim.

Notice that all claims are through female descent, which may explain why there is no clear heir.

The English claims   *Lady Catherine Grey.* Her mother was Frances Brandon, whose mother was Henry VIII's sister Mary. Her elder sister Jane was manipulated into exercising this claim, to her sorrow. Dies in 1568.

Her sons: *Thomas* (b. 1561) and *Edward* (b. 1563) Seymour. Catherine Grey's sons by the earl of Hertford, though the clandestine marriage was declared invalid by a special commission in 1562.

Lady Mary Grey. Younger sister to Catherine Grey. "Crouchback Mary" (said to be dwarfish and horribly ugly) was never seriously considered, although understood by many to be heir presumptive after her sister's death. Dies in 1578, without issue. She's the one who married the very tall serjeant porter.

Lady Margaret (Clifford) Stanley, Countess of Derby. Her mother was Eleanor Brandon, Frances's younger sister. Granddaughter to Mary Tudor. Next in line after the Grey girls, according to the Will. Dies 1596. Her sons maintain the claim:

- Lord Ferdinando Stanley. Eldest son. 1555–1594.
- William Stanley. Younger son. 1561–1630.

Henry Hastings, Earl of Huntington. His mother was Katherine Pole, a descendant of Edward III, and thus the last Plantagenet heir. Claim displaced by the rise of the Tudors, but still valid, especially since he is a man. Supported by Dudley and Norfolk. Dies childless in 1571.

Lady Margaret (Douglas) Stewart, Countess of Lennox. Her mother was Henry VIII's sister Margaret. Quarreled with Henry over religion, and he disinherited her. Dies 1578. *The Scottish claims*

Her son, *Charles Stewart, Earl of Lennox.* Dies 1577 (predeceasing his mother) but not before marrying Elizabeth Cavendish, Bess of Hardwick's daughter

His daughter, *Arbella Stewart.* She was brought up by her grandmothers to think of herself as the Queen's heiress. 1575–1615.

Mary Stuart, Queen of Scots. Her grandmother was Henry VIII's sister Margaret. Dies 1587.

Her son, *James VI, King of Scots.* Born 1568. Declared the Winner in 1603, when he becomes James I of England.

Not all of these people are contenders at the same time. Catherine Grey dies the year King James is born, for example. Of the English, only William Stanley and Arbella Stuart outlive the Queen. *Order of play*

Can't tell the players without a scorecard?

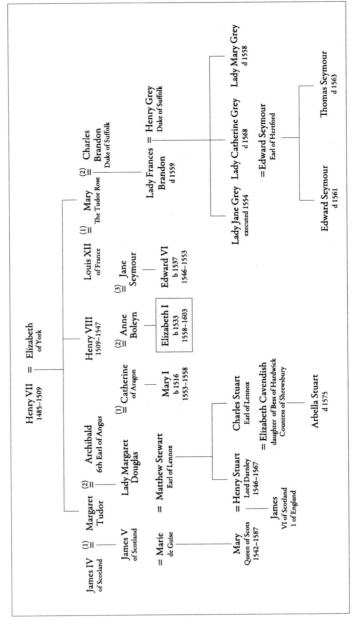

The Tudor succession. Source: Williams: All the Queen's Men

Filling the Time

As we know, there is nothing as dangerous as a bored nobleman (unless it's an idle soldier). These are some of the ways—
besides hunting—that a courtier at Court might fill his or her time.

Gossip, of course. But, like flirting, you can do that anywhere,
especially while doing almost any of the following.

Tennis is popular. It's played indoors or in a high-walled out-
door court. (The grass court comes into use in 1591.) The ball is
made of leather and stuffed with hair. Feel free to wager, sometimes for high stakes.

In *jeu de paume* there are no rackets; you hit the ball with
the palm of your hand over a tasseled rope stretched across the
center of the court.

Other sports include *bowls* (lawn bowling) for which Henry
VIII set up an alley at Whitehall. Bowling alleys exist about
London for ordinary people, too.

Also *shuttlecock* (like badminton), archery, billiards, hunting
and riding, wrestling, and political maneuvering.

Playing at bowls

Pall Mall has probably not yet come to England, but is popular in France and Scotland. It is not exactly croquet, so you can do what you like with the mallet and balls in the prop box.

Attend the *theatre*. This is in the afternoons, since there is no artificial lighting.

There are no *playhouses* until 1576; before that, the performance is very likely in an inn yard.

Young gentlemen of appearance can, for an extra fee, have their chairs put right up on the stage. Ladies attend, but are usually veiled or in masks.

There is a different play every day; perhaps a dozen plays (or more) in a repertory season.

Have the players in. Have them bring the play to your house. Count the silverware before they leave. Make sure you know who their patron is. Try to avoid performances of *Richard II* (with its deposition scene) and other controversial works, just in case. Do not sell tickets.

Food & Your Life Style

I N general, people eat two meals a day.
    Dinner is around midday, say 11:00 or 12:00.

Supper in the evening, about 5:00 or 6:00.

Husbandmen and others whose work is never done may have their supper as late as 9:00.

It is better to refer to having dinner instead of lunch or even luncheon. Invite people to dine with you, or ask "Where shall we dine today?"

Schoolboys, working people, and housewives get up around 5 or 6 AM, or even earlier.

These people certainly do not wait till 11:00 to eat. Breakfast is simply a matter of breaking one's fast on arising or on the way out the door, and is not considered a meal. It is certainly not understood to be "the most important meal of the day."

At Court, depending on the day's activities, or last night's, you probably arise somewhat later, and have a little bread and ale while being fussed over by your servants as they get you dressed and barbered, made-up and perfumed, and so on.

Of course, if (like a personal servant or a Lady of the Bedchamber) you are in charge of getting someone else dressed, you get up before they do. And *your* servants get up even earlier. Which may be one reason why the kitchens at Court never close.

A gentleman often has his dinner "out", either eating at an *ordinary* or buying food at a cook shop and taking it home. An ordinary is both the tavern that serves a daily fixed-price meal—plate of stew, loaf of bread, pot of ale—and the meal itself.

A gentleman who can't cadge a dinner invitation may say he is "dining with Duke Humphrey tonight."

In town, many houses have no proper kitchen. You may cook over the hearth, or prepare food and take it to a cook shop, and pick it up later, ready to eat. Few homes have their own oven, so you may make up your own bread but take it to a baker who, for a fee, will bake it for you.

Since we do not yet have tea, we do not yet have Tea Time.

More of What We Eat

H ERE *are some lists of period foods available for your dinner table.*

Vegetables   Garlic, asparagus, peas, spinach, eggplant, onions, cabbage, carrots, mustard, leeks, lettuce, endive, lentils, celery, parsnips, beets, broad beans, turnips, radishes, artichokes

An artichoke

Apples, plums, quinces, sloes, currants, lemons, oranges, dates, *Fruits and*
apricots, melons, sesame, wardons, almonds, strawberries, *nuts*
limes, grapes, prunes, gooseberries, figs, olives, mulberries,
pomegranates, cherries, raisins, hazelnuts, walnuts

DOMESTIC ANIMALS: Beef, veal, pork, chicken, duck, rabbit, *Meat and*
goat. Also swan, peacock, goose, pigeon, doves. Swans were *fowl*
fairly common in the Thames, and not especially an upper class
item.

WILD ANIMALS: Deer, boar, rabbit (or coney), quail, bus-
tard, curlew, plover, cormorant, badger, hedgehog, heron, crane,
pheasant, woodcock, partridge, etc.

FISH: Eels, pike, perch, trout, sturgeon, cod, haddock, ling, *Fish*
conger, plaice, roche, carp, salmon, porpoise, etc.

Snack Foods

S WEETS are commonly flavored with one or more of ginger,
nutmeg, mace, cloves, anise, coriander, rose water, sherry
(sack), almond and saffron.

MARZIPAN OR MARCHPANE: Almond paste that is sweetened,
colored, and made into shapes, often very elaborate ones.

GINGERBREAD: Both the crisp, cookie kind and the cake.
The familiar gingerbread men are called *gingerbread husbands.*
The cake form may be originally German or Dutch. In Germany, gingerbread is a common traveller's breakfast, accompanied
by brandy.

FRUIT PIES: Sweetened with sugar, thickened with almond
milk.

Sweet cakes (or cates) of various kinds.

Puddings: This means more than just dessert.

Daryole (cheesecakes) and custards.

Pretzels and bagels are both period in the Germanies.

More Things to Do

Still bored? Here are some more activities to occupy your days at Court.

Take lessons. There are plenty of professional fencing masters and dancing masters. (Sometimes they're the same people.)

Dancing lessons are important to keep up on the latest dances and latest steps, which you are expected to know.

The lute master

You might find a master to keep up your skills at the lute or the virginals or other refined instrument.

Brush up your French, Italian, or Spanish. Castiglione says one should be seen to be good at these languages. He's Italian, he should know.

Embroider. Like gossip, you can do this nearly anywhere. Ladies may gather in the garden, or in the Queen's Privy Chamber, or some other well-lighted room to do this. You might do it while watching a friend or family member take a lute lesson or sit for a portrait.

Play cards, chess, tables (backgammon) or draughts (checkers, pronounced *drafts*). Card games include Primero, Tarocho or Trumps, and many others.

Prepare a presentation, such as an elaborate masque. One must rehearse, after all.

Visit your tailor. This can take hours, especially if you take along some friends.

Sit for a portrait. The painter will make several visits, or you may visit him. You approve his sketches and his progress, and promise to pay the bill. A miniature by Hilliard will set you back about £40.

Visit the bear pit. Bear- (or bull-) baiting consists of letting a pack of crazed hounds loose on a chained bear (or bull), and watching from a safe distance while the beasts fight. Very popular. Almost as good as a public hanging. Even the Queen thinks this is great fun. One of the most famous of these bears is called Sackerson.

Practice riding at the ring and other tourney sports. The Queen loves a hardy man.

Sing. Like dancing, this has to be practiced, especially since some madrigals are quite difficult. The English are famous as sight-readers.

Says William Byrd:

First, it is a knowledge easily taught and quickly learned where there is a good master and an apt scholar.

2. The exercise of singing is delightful to nature and good to preserve the health of Man.

3. It doth strengthen all parts of the breast, and doth open the pipes.

4. It is a singular good remedy for a stuttering and stammering in the speech.

5. It is the best means to procure a perfect pronunciation, and to make a good orator.

6. It is the only way to know where Nature hath bestowed the benefit of a good voice, which gift is so rare as there is not one among a thousand that hath it: and in many that excellent gift is lost because they want [lack] Art to express Nature.

7. There is not any music of instruments whatsoever comparable to that which is made of the voices of Men, where the voices are good, and the same well sorted and ordered.

8. The better the voice is, the meeter it is to honour and serve God therewith: and the voice of Man is chiefly to be employed to that end.

> *Omnis spiritus laudet Dominum*
> *Since singing is so good a thing,*
> *I wish all men would learn to sing.*

Source   William Byrd, *Psalms, Sonnets, and songs of sadness and piety,* 1588.

Still More Things to Do

T RY reading.

Practically everyone is literate (with the odd exception of the 1st earl of Pembroke). Also, most people read out loud, even in company.

Councilors and border wardens and generals have reports to read. Or you may have reports from your steward(s) to consider.

Others may spend time with the Classics (Greek and Latin) or modern authors: Montaigne's *Essays*, if your French is good. Or Cervantes, if you have any Spanish. Castiglione, if you have kept up your Italian. If not, you can read Thomas Hoby's translation of *The Courtier* in 1561.

Chaucer is popular, as are other romances. Aubrey said the countess of Pembroke had the works of Chaucer "at her fingers' ends."

And there are devotional books (as well as the Bible) for both Catholics and protestants.

Sending messages is exactly like calling or texting someone on the phone.

Writing letters

People do it all day in all directions, whether around the Palace, to the house next door, across the city, or out to the countryside.

These may be no more than brief notes, inquiring after health or inviting to dine, reminding you of favors owed, or notifying you that the Queen has decided to hunt your deer park next week.

In international commerce, most correspondence is conducted in French; diplomacy, in Latin.

Writing
poetry   One does not publish, but one's poems may circulate in manuscript among friends. That's how the sonnets of Shakespeare, Sidney, and others originally appeared. (Viral poetry?)

Translation
and other
study   Not merely for students and professionals, this is open to ladies as well as gentlemen. Well-known lady scholars include the countess of Pembroke and the baroness Lumley.

Mildred, Lady Burghley and the other daughters of Anthony Coke were also notably learned ladies. Do not call them "bluestockings" as that term won't be available till about 1790.

&c.   AND of course, depending on your age, sex, and inclination:

- Walking in the gardens
- Going to the shops
- Having your fortune told
- Visiting friends
- Dining
- Negotiating a marriage contract
- Planning your daughter's wedding
- Having tradesmen in to show you their wares
- Seeing a physician
- Disciplining your servants
- Hanging out in taverns
- Gambling, and patronizing various low establishments on the wrong side of town.

Paying the Servants

O RDINARY household servants are hired at an annual wage and paid by the quarter (on Quarter Days). Most such servants earn between £2 and £5 per year, not adjusting for vails and fines.

They also get bed and board and 2 or 3 suits of livery clothing per year.

Some servant wages for 1550, Ingatestone Hall, Essex, the country manor of Privy Secretary Sir William Petre:

The laundress, cook, butler, and the children's nurse were paid 10s each. *By the quarter*

The youngest housemaid got 5s, as did a part-time brewer.

The gardeners got 10s 6d each.

Bailiff: 11s/8d (£2/6s/8d per year)

Best paid: Chaplain: 13s/4d (£3/5s per year)

The Queen's maids of honour get a stipend of £40 per year. *By the year*

The Privy Secretary gets an annual income of £100, exclusive of fees, fines, bribes, douceurs, etc.

By contrast, in 1568 the Queen's laundress, Mistress Taylor, gets £4 per year, with an extra £6 for her livery gown.

Royal accounts show the Queen's household expenses at about £55,000 per year. It helps that so much of the expense of Progress is born by her hosts along the way.

For the period of July 1566 to April 1567, her master embroiderer, David Smith, was paid £203/15/7 from the Privy Purse to cover his salary and all expenses of his office. His assistant, William Middleton, got £25/11/11.

Henslow's Diary shows actors being paid 10s. a week in town and 5s. on the road in the 1590s. Actors!

Erickson: *The First Elizabeth* *Sources*
Emmison: *The Tudor Secretary*
Henslow's *Diary*

Staffing a Great Household

Anthony
Viscount
Montague,
1595

From *A Book of Orders and Rules*, edited from the original ms. by Sir Sibbald David Scott, Bart., in *Sussex Archaeological Collections*, vol. vii, London 1854.

"*A Book of Orders and Rules, established by me Anthony Viscount Montague for the better direction and gouvernment of my household and family…*"

1. Steward of the Household
2. Comptroller
3. High steward of the Courts
4. Auditor
5. General Receiver

6. Solicitor
7. Other principal officers
8. Secretary
9. Gentlemen Ushers
10. Carver
11. Sewer (server)
12. Gentlemen of the Chamber
13. Gentlemen of Horse
14. Gentlemen waiters
15. Marshall of the Hall
16. Clerk of the Kitchen

17. Yeomen of the Great Chamber
18. Usher of the Hall
19. Chief cook

20. Yeomen of the chamber
21. Clerk of the Officer's Chambers
22. Yeoman of the Horse
23. Yeoman of the Cellar
24. Yeoman of the Ewery
25. Yeoman of the Pantry
26. Yeoman of the Buttery
27. Yeoman of the Wardrobe
28. Yeoman waiters

29. Second cook, and the rest
30. Porter
31. Granator
32. Bailiff

33. Baker

34. Brewer

35. Grooms of the Great
    Chamber

36. Almoner

37. Scullery man

In 1604 the Earl of Hertford's embassy to Brussels included 20 knights, 2 barons, and 7 gentlemen, plus their servants to a total of 90.

An ambassadorial household: 1604

And in the earl's personal train:

 2 chaplains

 1 surgeon

 6 pages

 1 steward

 1 physician

 3 wardrobers

 1 secretary

 1 apothecary

16 gentlemen waiters

 1 gentleman of the horse

 8 musicians

30 yeoman waiters

 2 gentlemen ushers

 8 trumpeters

30 kitchen, buttery & pantry staff

 1 harbinger

 6 footmen

 4 gentlemen of the chamber

 1 master of carriages and 10 lackeys

Some fines and rules in Sir John Harington's house

- A servant must not be absent from morning or evening meals or prayers lest he be fined 2 pence for each time.
- Any servant late to dinner will be fined 2 pence.
- Any man waiting table without a trencher in his hand, except for good excuse, will be fined 1 penny.
- For each oath, a servant to be fined a penny.
- Any man provoking another to strike, or striking another, is liable to dismissal.
- For a dirty shirt on Sunday or a missing button, the fine to be sixpence.
- Any man leaving a door open that he found shut to be fined one penny unless he could show good cause.
- After 8:00 AM no bed must be found unmade and no fireplace or candle box left uncleaned, or the fine to be one penny.
- The hall must be cleaned in an hour's time.
- The whole house must be swept and dusted each Friday.

Proverbs & Wise Sayings

On husbands and wives

A WOMAN fit to be a man's wife is too good to be his servant.

A wife, a spaniel, a walnut tree: The more you beat them, the better they be.

Women commend a modest man but like him not.

On character

Red wise
Brown trusty
Pale envious
Black lusty

Age and wedlock tames man and beast.

Everyone knows

Many kiss the child for its nurse's sake.

You are as seasonable as snow in Summer.

Three may keep counsel if two be away.

Four pints of ale at a meal is three too many.

A bow long bent at last waxeth weak.

God sends meat, the devil sends cooks.

Need hath no law.

The crow thinketh her own birds fairest.

A trusty servant's portrait you would see,

The perfect servant?

    This emblematic figure we'll survey.

The porker's snout—not nice in diet shows;

The padlock's shut—no secret he'll disclose;

Patient the ass—his master's wrath will bear;

Swiftness in errand—the stag's feet will declare;

Alluded his left hand—apt to labour saith;

The vest—his neatness; open hand—his faith;

Girt with his sword, his shield upon his arm,

Himself and master he'll protect from harm.

> — *Graffiti on the kitchen wall*
> *at Winchester College,*
> *dated 1563*

What Every Schoolboy Knows

IN general, only boys go to school. A girl's education is accomplished at home, although it usually includes reading and arithmetic.

Of course, noble children get their education at home, from private tutors. Some pay more attention than others.

It is understood that students must have their education beaten into them, like their manners and deportment. Parents tend to support this theory.

Public education refers to going out to school, as opposed to being tutored privately. It does not mean they are paid for out of public funds. Hence, the great "public schools" like Eton.

The school day begins at 7:00 AM in winter or 6:00 AM in summer. After prayers, they work till about 9:00 when they are permitted to break their fast, then they work till 11:00. Dinner is from 11:00 to 1:00. The school day ends at 5:00 or 5:30 PM.

Petty schools The most elementary level of schooling is called *petty school*. You learn to read and write in English and do sums, but the main idea is to prepare you for a grammar school.

The petty school is often run by a young wife who teaches the local children in her home for a small fee, like the "dame schools" of Colonial days. All other teachers are men.

The principal study of a *grammar school* is Latin grammar, using   *Grammar*
Lily's *Grammar* as the basic text. Also old standards by Alain   *schools*
de Lille and Robert Grosseteste, supplemented by Plautus,
Terence, and Seneca as classical sources. Any history, literature,
or drama is mainly a vehicle for illustrating the grammar.

The function of the grammar school is to prepare you for
university, where courses are conducted in Latin, even after
the Reformation. Music, modern languages, and science are
irrelevant.

Latin is also the language of international affairs, and men
of affairs are expected to be able to communicate in it. Or em-
ploy someone who does. Anyone who wants to make his way in
the world must have at least a working knowledge of Latin.

Some educators take a slightly broader view. The young earl
of Essex followed this daily programme while a ward in Burghley's house:

7:00 – 7:30	Dancing
7:30 – 8:00	Breakfast
8:00 – 9:00	French
9:00 – 10:00	Latin
10:00 – 10:30	Writing and Drawing
10:30 – 1:00	Prayers, Recreation, Dinner
1:00 – 2:00	Cosmography
2:00 – 3:00	Latin
3:00 – 4:00	French
4:00 – 4:30	Writing
4:30 – 5:30	Prayers, Recreation, Supper

Notice that there is time for writing but not for spelling. After all, what good is a man who can only spell his name one way?

Sources   Lacey: *Robert, Earl of Essex*
Rowse: *Southampton, Shakespeare's Patron*

Classical References

The Muses   THE Muses are the nine daughters of Zeus and Memory, who preside over the arts and philosophy. They reside on Mount Helicon, and are under the patronage of Apollo.

In the Classical period, the following names and assignments were accepted, although they may vary (and may be useful when planning Masques).

Calliope	(ka-lie'-oh-pee)	Poetry
Clio	(klee'-oh)	History
Polyhymnia	(polly-him'-nee-a)	Mime
Euterpe	(you-ter'-pee)	Instrumental music
Terpsichore	(terp-sik'-oh-ree)	Dance
Erato	(er-at'-o)	Choral music
Melpomene	(mel-pom'-in-ee)	Tragedy
Thalia	(thay'-lee-a)	Comedy
Urania	(you-rain'-ee-a)	Astronomy

Other deities   *Morpheus* is the winged god of dreams, one of the children of Sleep.

Jupiter (or *Jove*) is the king of the Gods in the Roman pantheon. His Greek counterpart is *Zeus*. Both are into thunderbolts. Yes, we comfortably interchange Greek and Roman names. Hey, it's the Renaissance.

Mars (Ares) is the god of war. Note that Ares the god is *not* Aries the ram of the Zodiac.

Venus (Aphrodite) is understood to be the goddess of Love; she is married to Vulcan, who forges thunderbolts for Jupiter in a volcano.

Her son is *Cupid (Eros)*.

Vulcan (Hephaestus) is lame and ugly. He once caught Venus *in flagrante* with Mars!

Minerva (Athena) is the goddess of Wisdom and Battle.

Iris is the goddess of the Rainbow.

Hermes (her'-meez) is the messenger of the gods, and has special winged sandals for speed. He is also patron of commerce, and speeds travelers on their way.

His son is pastoral *Pan*, who frolics with the wild beasts and makes us panic.

Ganymede (gan'-ee-meed) is the cup bearer of the gods, and thus any young boy or girl serving at table, or a page.

Grimal: *The Dictionary of Classical Mythology*   *Source*

Letter Writing

T HE Elizabethans and their friends do not seem to have settled on any one form of salutation for letters, such as "Dear Mom." Overall, the conventions of letter writing are as formal as speaking in person, or perhaps even more so!

Perhaps the most nearly standard brief opening is something like: *My humble duty remembered...*

Salutations are often long and full of blessings and humility. The date is usually at the end of the letter.

The address or instructions for delivery on the outside of a letter are called the *direction*.

In these examples, I have left the punctuation more or less intact, except to replace a virgule (/) with a comma and a semi-colon with a period to indicate a full stop. They also used commas with considerable abandon, which I have restrained, and they do ramble on. The word [*sig.*] indicates the signature.

Numbers are frequently given in lower case Roman numerals, with the last "i" in a number written with a tail, like a "j". For example, *viij March*.

Short notes for specail occasions

To a very noble patroness

Right honourable, with our most humble and dutiful thanks for your ladyship's bountiful goodness towards us all times, my wife and I have made bold to present your Honourable Ladyship with such poor and homely things for a simple new year's gift as this place can afford, beseeching that according to your ladyship's accustomed goodness, you will vouchsafe them in good part; and we shall pray most earnestly to God almighty to send your honourable ladyship many happy healthful new years.

The almighty preserve your ladyship in health and send you a good and comfortable end of all your great troubles and griefs. Wynfield this Tuesday the v of November at viij of the clock at night 1588

Your honour's most dutiful bound obedient servant

[*sig.*]

The Privy Council to Master William More
[*The direction reads: To our very loving friend W. More, Esquire*]

After our very hearty recommendations we have thought meet, for good consideration, to require you to signify unto

us by your private letter, whether the Earl of Southampton, at present remaining in your house, do come to Common Prayer or not; and in case he have not so done already, then we require you as of yourself to move and persuade him thereunto, and of that he shall do or hath done, and shall answer thereupon, we pray you to advertise us with convenient speed. And so we bid you farewell. From Windsor, the xviij of October, 1570
    Your loving friends,
        [signed by members of the Privy Council]

To a relative

Good uncle, after my heartiest commendations to you and to mine aunt…

Opening lines can also be brief

To a friend

After my very hearty commendations…

To a mother

My humble duty remembered…

To a noble man

Right Worshipful, My humble duty remembered, hoping in the Almighty of your health and prosperity which on my knees I beseech him long to continue…

To a noble relative

Your lordship's assured friend and kinsman
    [sig.]

Closing lines can be either brief or fulsome

To an equal who has done (or perhaps been asked) a favor

Thus indebted to you for your pains taken for me, I bid you farewell. Sprowston, this xx of April. Your friend,
    [sig.]

To a friend

> Thus I commit you to god's good protection. From Hampton
> Court the 2ᵈ of January 1592. Your very assured friend
>   [*sig.*]

To a parent

> And thus with commendations from my partner and sister
> with thanks for our good cheer, and not forgetting Aunt Let-
> tyce, with blessing to Mall, nephews Lewis, Harvey, and Nick,
> and Nan, with our humble duty to my mother we commit you
> to God this Saturday 17 December
>   [*sig.*]

To a kinsman

> Your very assured loving friend and kinsman
>   [*sig.*]

To the Queen

> And so I bid your Grace and the rest heartily farewell. From
> my house in the Strand this xix of March, 1596, Your assured
> loving friend
>   [*sig.*]

To a noble mother

> And so humbly craving your ladyship's daily blessing to us
> both, we most humbly take our leave, Tutbery the last of De-
> cember 1605
>   Your ladyship's humble and obedient son
>   [*sig.*]

To a brother

> I pray you remember my duty to my good mother. This with
> my kindest commend to you and my good sister, wishing you
> all happiness, I rest your loving sister

[sig.]
Court at Woodstock
this 26th August 1599

To a mother

With the remembrance of my humble duty unto you, I humbly
take my leave and rest,
Your dutiful and obedient son,
[sig.]

Dawson and Kennedy-Skipton: *Elizabethan Handwriting*   *Sources*
Rowse: *Southampton, Shakespeare's Patron*

Random Bits & Bobs

A CTORS sometimes have access to very good second-hand   *Theatrical*
clothes to use as costumes. From an inventory of the Lord   *costumes*
Chamberlain's Men (Shakespeare's company) comes this gaudy
note in Henslow's Diary: "Bought: a doublet of white satin laid
thick with gold lace and a pair of round hose [slops] of cloth of
silver, the panes laid with gold lace."

Although Puritan Philip Stubbs complains of people wearing   *Jewelry &*
rings on every finger of the hand, the middle finger is not used. *decoration*
This is apparently evidence of a common notion that the mid-
dle finger is for fools.

Among the nastier elements of that very white face make-up
are antimony and lead. It all looks better by candlelight.

The legal, Parliamentary, and university year (Oxford) is divid-   *School*
ed into four sessions or *terms*, designated by the feast day which *terms*
begins them:

Michaelmas (October–December)
Hilary (January–April)
Easter (April–May)
Trinity (June–July)

Medicine   Medicines prescribed by physicians are made up by an apothecary.

The apothecaries belong to the Grocers Company and have to serve an apprenticeship.

The weather   The expression St. Martin's Summer refers to what Americans call "Indian summer": an unusually summery period sometime in the fall.

St. Martin's Day is November 11.

Seasons   The seasons are understood to begin not on the equinox or solstice but when the weather and land actually change:

Spring	February 1	Candlemas
Summer	May 1	May Day (another Lady Day)
Fall	August 1	Lammas
Winter	November 1	All Hallows/All Saints

Sources   Henslow's *Diary*
Hutton: *Seasons of the Sun*
Kuntz: *Rings for the Finger*

More Fashionable Vocabulary

A nightgown is called a *night rail*, presuming you sleep in something besides your shift or your nudity. A veil is also a *head rail*.

The ties on your shirt (or whatever) are called *points*. The metal tags on the ends of the points are called *aiglets* (agg'-lets).

Your sleeves are *trussed* (tied) to your doublet with points.

Your hoopskirt is a *farthingale*.

Ruffs come as a suite—collar and cuffs.

Pockets are period. So are functional buttonholes. Don't let anyone tell you otherwise.

Fabric comes on a *folder* instead of on a bolt.

An account for the making of a man's doublet (including sleeves), breeches, and cloak in 1595 shows the *tailor* being paid 14 shillings for his work. *Fashionable expenses*

The cost for *materials* came to almost £14 for velvet, fustian (for lining), double taffeta, gold braid and gold lace (at 10s. an ounce), silk for lining and hose, and 3 dozen buttons for the doublet.

Good velvet went for 12s per yard in 1536 and 26s per yard (24–30" wide) in 1565.

Seed pearls, bought in bulk for use on gowns, cost a penny apiece.

Virtue & Vice, or vice versa

Vices   ACCORDING to the Church, and thus to Western man, the most deadly sins are these. Violations involving them may be great (mortal) or small (venial).

- Sloth (or Despair)
- Envy
- Lust
- Covetousness (or Greed)
- Anger
- Gluttony
- and of course, Pride

In one point of view at least, all these are variations on Pride. Judas's sin of Despair, for example, was prideful in maintaining that his sin was so great that even God could not forgive it, which furthermore presumes that God's power is limited.

Virtues   The Virtues come in several categories: Moral, Worldly, and Divine.

The chief *moral* virtues are Prudence, Justice, Fortitude, Temperance, Religion, Obedience, Chastity, and Humility. The first four of these are also called "natural" virtues.

The *worldly* virtues are Understanding, Wisdom, Knowledge, Prudence, and Art (applied Knowledge).

The *divine* virtues are Faith, Hope, and Charity.

Passions   The Passions are:

- Joy
- Despair
- Sorrow
- Choler (anger)

- Fear
- Hope
- Boldness
- Desire
- Love
- Eschewing (self-sacrifice)
- Hatred

A Classical Education

IF you have a university education (or know someone who has), you should be at least slightly familiar with the following course of study, which has been in place since medieval times. Courses in beer and mayhem are supplementary.

These names and titles will at least allow you to say "well, as Boethius says..."

In these areas, the authority is always Aristotle:

In the faculty of arts

Logical or Rational Philosophy
Organon, Categories, On Interpretation, Analytics, etc.

Moral Philosophy
Ethics, Politics, Rhetoric, Poetics

Natural Philosophy, or Natural History
Physical Discourse, On the Heavens, On the Soul, On Parts of Animals, Meteorologics, etc.

THE TRIVIUM

In the liberal arts

Grammar
Priscian, Donatus, Villedieu, Cassiodorus, and some pagan and early Christian writers.

Rhetoric
Quintillian, Cicero, Eberhard de Bethune

Logic
Porphyry, Gilbert de la Poré, Hispanus

THE QUADRIVIUM

Arithmetic
John of Holywood, John of Pisa

Geometry
Euclid, Boethius

Music
Boethius, Jehan de Muris of Paris (*Ars novae musicae*, 1319), Plato's *Timaeus*, Aristoxenos

Astronomy
Gerard de Cremona

In the faculty of law The principal Latin authorities are:

In civil law
Corpus Juris Civilis, the *Code*, the *Pandects* (a digest), the *Institutes*, the *Novellae*

In canon (church) law
Gratian, Bartholomew, Pope Gregory IX, Pope Boniface VIII, *Constitutiones Clementiae*

In the faculty of theology The Bible, Peter Lombard, Church Fathers and great doctors of the church such as Origen, Aquinas & Augustine

In the faculty of medecine Hippocrates, Galen, Arabic and Jewish medical texts, Theodore of Lucca, Lanfranc, Chauliac

Isidore of Seville
  Etymologiae (On language) and *Sententiae* (Maxims)

Rabanus Maurus
  On the Universe and *On the Instruction of the Clergy*

(Emperor) Frederick II
  The Falcon Book

Dame Juliana Berners
  The Boke of St Albans (on hunting), *Treatyse of fysshynge wyth an Angle* (fishing)

Dinner at Cowdray House, 1595

Edited from Sir S. D. Scott, Bart., in *Sussex Archæological Collections,* 1926.

The writer points out that although this is late reign, the house is stubbornly Catholic, and the new young Viscount Montague (age 22) is interested in preserving the stately habits of his grandfather's household, to which he is heir.

Ten o'clock has just struck, and the household is mustering in the Hall, it being covering time, or the hour for preparing the tables for dinner. The Steward in his gown is standing at the uppermost part of the Hall, surrounded by most of his chief officers and some visitors, perhaps also some travelers, "strangers" who have availed themselves of His Lordship's hospitality.

The tables are neatly covered with white cloths, salt cellars, and trenchers, under the supervision of the Chief Usher. The Yeomen of the Ewery and Pantry, conducted by the Yeoman Usher, pass through to the great Dining Chamber. When they arrive in the middle of that room they bow reverently (although no one else be present) and do the same on approaching the table.

The Usher, kissing his hand, places it on the center of the table indicating to his subordinate where the cloth is to be laid.

The Yeoman of the Pantry steps forth and places salt and trenchers for my lord and lady, with bread, knives, and spoons, making a little bow as each item is laid down.

The trio then reverence and retire.

Next comes the Yeoman of the Cellar who dresses the sideboard with wines, flagons, drinking cups and such vessels as are in his charge. The Yeoman of the Buttery follows and brings up beer and ale, and arranges the pewter pots, jugs, and so forth on the sideboard. It now being dinner time, the Gentleman Usher proceeds to take his Lord's commands.

Having received his orders, he sees that the carver and server wash their hands and have clean cloths for their arms. The Usher of the Hall standing at the screen [the decorative barrier to the kitchen] calls out, "Gentlemen and Yeoman, Wait upon the Server for my Lord!", half a dozen gentlemen and yeomen at least following him to the sideboard.

When they return, each carrying a dish, the Usher calls, "By your leave, my masters," and all who are present in the Hall stand while the Lord's dinner processes through the Hall to the dining chamber, where it is met by the Gentleman Usher, who sees the dishes placed on the table.

The Viscount, having been informed by the Gentleman Usher that all is ready, comes forth leading his lady, followed by her gentlewomen.

When dinner is over and the table cloth removed, the Gentleman Usher comes forth with a towel, and basins and ewers are produced for the lords' and ladies' ablutions.

The attendants are dismissed and depart with reverences, to take their dinners with all those who have been occupied in the service for the "second sitting" in the Hall.

While they are so engaged, the Steward and those who sat at his table repair to the Lord's dining chamber and remain in attendance until the Gentlemen Waiters return, and all await the rising of the Viscount from his table.

The assemblage is now dispersed. Those who have leisure and desire it are at liberty to call for cards in the Hall, which the Yeoman officers provide, each player bestowing a gratuity in the "playing box" for this service, the contents of which are proportionately divided.

More Wedding Customs

A bride is not expected to wear a white dress. It can be any fashionable or current color and cut. White as a color for brides does not become entrenched until the 19th century.

Depending on the social status of the families, the bride might have a new gown made, or simply wear her best clothes, freshened up with new ribbons or flowers. She certainly wears flowers in her hair.

However, the dress is a gown like any other. It is not a unique style, unsuitable for any other use and sentimentally preserved for later generations. Even a specially-made gown would become part of the lady's ordinary wardrobe.

The costs of the wedding festivities are generally borne by

the bride's father. In less prosperous neighborhoods, the food may be supplied by the neighbors, pot-luck style or cooked in the *church house*.

Sometimes the costs of the day are defrayed by holding a *bride ale*, usually in the churchyard. There the bride sells cups of ale for as much as her friends will pay. This is not the same thing as a "bridal shower", and is not limited to female attendance.

Various social elements of the parish also hold church ales occasionally as a fund-raising event.

Crying the banns   The intention to marry must be announced in the church three times; that is, on three consecutive Sundays or holy days, in the same parish.

If the two people live in different parishes, the banns must be read in both. This allows time for any objections to be raised or pre-contracts to be discovered.

Any marriage not published before-hand is considered clandestine, and illegal.

There is no set form of wedding invitation. People do, however, send messages to their friends and relations, and gifts are cheerfully received. If the wedding is at Court, everyone simply understands they are expected.

The bridal procession   Any bridesmaids (*i.e.*, the bride's maids) help the bride to prepare, then they, the bride, the groom, the families, and all the guests assemble, and go in procession from the house or houses to the church.

The bridal procession is generally noisy, accompanied by musicians, laughter, and bawdy jokes. Town councils have been known to complain about the noise and general disorder.

If the groom is not part of the procession, he meets the bride either at the side door of the church or at the altar.

They all enter the church at once and stand through the ritual.

The wedding is always a religious ceremony, conducted by a minister. No getting married in the Registry, or at a Justice of the Peace, and no running off to Gretna Green.

The words of the English service are essentially the same then as now, since they come from the Book of Common Prayer of 1559.

Since the church is open, anyone can attend as long as there is room, although fairly strict social order is observed. Poorer neighbors, tenants, and passers by stand at the back.

For noble and other propertied families, the most significant part of a wedding day is the signing of the wedding contract, which sets out the terms of dowry, jointure, and other elements for the financial security of both parties. *Contract, dowry, jointure*

The dowry is an amount of money, goods, and property the bride brings to the marriage. It can also be called her marriage portion.

The jointure is an agreement by the groom's family to guarantee specific money, property and goods to the bride if her husband dies before she does, aside from or in addition to what is in his will. Sometimes this agreement is assured by promises from the family's friends.

Viscount Montague provided his daughter Mary, who became Countess to the 2nd earl of Southampton in 1567, with a dowry of £1,333.

In 1591, Lord Compton demanded a dowry of £10,000 plus the redeeming of an £18,000 mortgage on his land from Sir John

Spencer, Lord Mayor of London, whose daughter he wished to marry. Spencer fought it, but in the end, the marriage took place. This is not, however, the normal circumstance.

In many noble cases, the event is commemorated with individual portraits of the bride and groom, completed before the wedding. Many of the "unknown girl" pictures one finds were painted for such an occasion.

Some resources
Cressy: *Birth, Marriage, and Death*
Duffy: *Voices of Morebath*
Pearson: *Elizabethans at Home*
Stopes: *Southampton*

Keeping Christmas

A NOTE *of caution: Christmas customs are hard to pin down and harder still to identify as genuinely Elizabethan—that is, verifiably in use during the Elizabethan era. (The past is not all the same place.) With the shifts from Catholic to protestant and back and forth again, some customs were banned or simply stopped, revived, then abandoned. Here are some of the things we're sure of.*

> So now is come our joyful'st feast, Let every man be jolly.
> Each room with ivy leaves is drest, And every post with holly.
> Though some churls at our mirth repine,
> Round your foreheads garlands twine,
> Drown sorrow in a cup of wine, And let us all be merry.
> —George Wither (1588–1667)

The Christmas season or Christmastide runs the twelve days from 24 December to 6 January; that is, Christmas Eve to Epiphany or Twelfth Day. The evening of that day is called

Twelfth Night, and is the last party of
the season.

It is a festival season with only passing reference to religion, although in
Catholic reigns there are three Masses for Christmas Day, starting with
Matins.

Feasting, generosity, disguisings,
pageants, role-reversal, and silliness are
the principal elements. Also gambling,
especially card playing and tables. (Puritans do not approve.)

Hospitality is the rule. All who can do so furnish their tables *Hospitality*
with all the meats, marchpanes, pies, custards, and so on that
they can afford, and more.

Entertainments in the season include mummer's plays of
various kinds, often incorporating music and *morris dancing*
(also performed at May Day). The story of St. George and the
Dragon is especially popular. Morris dancers are regularly invited to perform at Court.

Such entertainments are meant for the whole manor or
household, including tenants; the whole village; or the whole
Court.

The Queen keeps Christmas most often at Greenwich Palace,
which is relatively small. Alternate locations in certain years
are Hampton Court (in 1568 and 1579) and Nonesuch Palace.

Court festivities, as at other times, include dancing, gambling, and plays.

The decorations about any house include holly, ivy, box, yew, *Greenery*
bay, laurel, holm oak, and in fact, anything still green. Both

church records and household accounts show money spent for holly and ivy to be brought in for the holiday.

In the church itself, along with the greenery, a wooden figure of the Christ Child sometimes rests on the altar. The "nativity scene" hasn't come to England from Italy yet.

Mistletoe grows only on oak and apple trees. It isn't mentioned in a Christmas context before 1622, at which time it seems a fond custom, not newly introduced, but we can't tell how far back its use in England goes, or if it was regional, or what. If it was common, it should be easy to find.

Kissing under the mistletoe has not yet become traditional, even in 1622.

Yule or Christmas log. The young men of the household go out on Christmas Eve and dress (trim) a log or block of wood from the central trunk of a tree specially chosen for the purpose. They drag it into the fireplace in the hall, where it is lit with a bit saved from last year's log, and is expected to burn all night.

Sensible people save pieces from the Christmas log through the next year to protect the house from fire.

Food   The most popular Christmas dinner is roast beef or brawn (roast pork) with mustard.

Also popular are mince pies, frumenty, plum porridge, and a Christmas pie of neat's tongue, eggs, sugar, lemon & orange peel, and spices.

> Good husband and huswife, now chiefly be glad,
> Things handsome to have, as they ought to be had.
> They both do provide, against Christmas do come,
> To welcome their neighbors, good cheer to have some.
> Good bread and good drink, a good fire in the hall,
> Brawn, pudding, and souse, and good mustard withal.

Beef, mutton, and pork, and good pies of the best,
Pig, veal, goose, and capon, and turkey well drest,
Cheese, apples and nuts, and good carols to hear
As then in the country is counted good cheer.
What cost to good husband, is any of this?
Good household provision only it is:
Of other the like, I do leave out a many,
That costeth the husband never a penny.
      —*from* Thomas Tusser, 500 *Points of Husbandry,* 1573

Hartley: *Lost Country Life*   *Sources*
Hubert: *Christmas in Shakespeare's England*
Hutton: *Seasons of the Sun*
Monson: "Elizabethan Holiday Customs"

Gifts at the New Year

N EW Year feasting and gift giving goes back to the Romans, who started the year on January 1. Although the legal year starts in March, the midwinter custom is too entrenched to change.

Gifts are given at New Year's, not on Christmas day. Such giving is mentioned in every full set of household accounts available between 1400–1550.

Christmas has not yet been personified, or associated with St Nicholas. No one in England expects to receive gifts from a supernatural agent such as Father Christmas or Santa Claus. However, you might hire a fool for the day, and give him that job.

Courtier's gifts given to the Queen include:

+ Gold coins in an embroidered pouch
+ Garments (sleeves, foreparts, partlets, suites of ruffs, etc.)
+ Sweet bags (scented, usually embroidered pillows, sometimes with a pocket for a coin)
+ Jewelled fan
+ Looking glass
+ Embroidered smock
+ Jewelry (for example, the Heneage jewel)

Gifts to the Queen from the royal household are often related to the office: a marzipan chessboard and chessmen from the Master Cook, a pot of green ginger from the doctor, a fancy meat knife from the Cutler, a gilded quince pie from the Sergeant of the Pastry, and so on.

From the Queen, a courtier can generally expect to receive a silver cover cup of a particular weight, delivered by messenger, or picked up on a voucher.

Schoolboys at Eton play games to win prizes, and make presents of verses to their masters and each other.

Among ordinary folk, according to Ben Jonson, gifts may include oranges, a bunch of rosemary, brooches, marzipan, and wine.

Prosperous citizens may send gifts of fowl or rabbits to the mayor, who will provide a feast in return (using the gifts, we presume).

In one account, the earl of Northumberland was awakened on New Year's morning by minstrels, followed by a fanfare of trumpets. He received his gifts, and then gave gifts to his household. He held a feast at noon, processing into the Hall in great state. He then watched a play followed by a bergomask, interspersed with pageants.

NOTE: The celebration of the day after Christmas as Boxing day is not recorded till 1621.

Hartley: *Lost Country Life*   Sources
Hutton: *Seasons of the Sun*
Monson: "Elizabethan Holiday Customs"

Good English Ale

Hops and heresy, bays and beer
All came to England in one year.
                              —old rhyme

ALE is made from barley, but it can be flavored with just about anything, including pepper, ivy, rosemary, bilberries, and lupines, among many other things. When it's flavored with hops, it becomes *beer*.

Andrew Boorde (c. 1452) tells us that "Ale is made of malt and water, and they the which do put any other thing to ale … except yeast, barm, and God's good doth sophisticate their ale…" He does not mean "sophisticate" as a good thing.

Hops were added to ale in England for the first time in the early 16th century, to keep it from going off.

Caxton tells us that "beer was made in England by beer brewers who were Flemings and Dutchmen." By now, we've pretty much stopped whinging that it "tastes foreign" and that it isn't "good English ale".

Brewing

Neither drink is any more than slightly effervescent so no frothy head to blow off, no bubbles to speak of.

Ale is the sweeter drink, but when it goes off it becomes syrupy and nasty. Hops make it bitter but also make it last longer in the barrel.

At market fairs, the *ale-conner* is an officer appointed by the steward of the Fair (and in larger towns by the *leet court*), to review the wholesomeness of bread, ale, and beer offered for sale, and ensure that it is sold at a fair price.

Beer's natural effects often lead to colorful names. The last two of these surely refer to the aftermath of too much time at the ale house.

- Huffcap
- The mad dog
- Merry-go-down
- Angel's food
- Dragon's milk
- Go-by-the-wall
- Stride wide

Beer drunk too soon is sour. Sour beer that has also suffered from the vagaries of weather, heat, and time is just vile. On Progress one year, the local brew was so awful that the Queen refused to drink it, and sent back to London for her own brewmaster.

In gentlemen's homes, brewing is usually done in March; thus references to March beer. The best beer is about a year old, and has had time to mellow.

Most other people are content to make beer once a month on brewing day. This small beer has less alcohol, but the hoppy bitterness is reduced enough to be a pleasant drink.

> Now bring us in good ale, good ale, and bring us in good ale.
> For our blessed Lady's sake, bring us in good ale.
> —15th century carol

Brewing is traditionally women's work. In a great house, the stillroom maid and sometimes the lady of the house take responsibility for providing beer for the household.

A housewife brews once a month for her own household's use. Her costs (in the 1570s) come to about 20 shillings for 3 hogsheads yield. If she does this for a living, as many widows do, she is an *alewife*.

The fermenting liquor is stirred with a *besom* (bundled

broom). When it is hung out to dry over a door or window, it shows the neighborhood that the new batch is ready. The "bush" in pub names like "The Bull and Bush" refers to this broom.

Other uses   Hops give a good yellow dye, and the young tops can be cooked with butter and eaten.

Sources   Chappell: *The Ballad Literature and Popular Music of the Olden Time*
Harrison: *Description of England 1577*
Hartley: *Lost Country Life*
Beer & Real Ale: A Brief History at http://www.pubs.com/
Workshop: Angela Grimes

More Measures

"It is to be lamented that one general measure is not in use through-out all England, but every market town hath in manner a several bushel. Such is the covetousness of many clerks of the market, that in taking view of measures they will always so provide that one and the same bushel shall either be too big or too little...so that divers unconscionable dealers have one measure to sell by and another to buy withal; the like also in weights."
—*in* Lost Country Life

T RADE goods of various kinds traditionally have their own customary measures, although some actual amounts are variable. A dozen is always 12, but barrels come in varying sizes.

A Scottish ell is about a yard (16 *nails* of two-and-a half inch-es), but an English ell is 45 inches (20 nails).

These	Are sold by the
Butter, beer, herring, salmon and other fish, eels, tar, pitch, gunpowder, wines	Barrel Firkin (smaller quantities)
Honey and other thick liquids	Bolle
Sackcloth, sailcloth, and quantities of haircloth	Bolt
Hay, straw, wood, lime, rushes	Cartload (In smaller quantities, rushes are sold by the creel or the shoulder load)
New coal, salt, quicklime, shells for making lime	Chaldron
A 7-pound weight of wool	Clove
Glass	Cradle
Hurdles, tanned hides, napkins, sheepskins, needles	Diker

These	Are sold by the
Candles (also sold by weight)	Dozen
Linen and small lengths of haircloth	Ell
Soft fruits	Frail

Sources   Harrison: *A Description of England*
            Hartley: *Lost Country Life*
            Orlin: *Elizabethan Households*

To Set a Fine Table

W E eat from *trenchers* (plates), usually with a spoon or simply fingers, assisted by a knife. A trencher is generally made of treen (wood) or pewter. The old habit of carving a plate from sturdy or twice-baked bread is no longer common.

Forks have not yet become popular in England, except as a tool for holding large pieces of meat while carving. People who

put a fork right into their mouths are either too, too fastidious, too Italianate, or terribly brave.

Napkins (not serviettes) are slung over the shoulder or arm, often secured with a pin—not tucked into the neck or laid on the lap.

Table linens are referred to as *napery*, and are the responsibility of the chief usher.

A well-set table is laid with a *carpet*, then a white damask cloth, trenchers, and bread (one loaf for every one or two diners).

In a fine house, a servant or two takes a ewer and basin to each diner so they can rinse their hands before eating. Another follows close behind with a cloth to dry the hands.

When the meal is finished, any *broken meats* that remain are given to the servants or distributed to the poor at the kitchen door.

The Steward & His Office

THE *management skills required to coordinate a great house and its staff are extraordinary. This list of duties is drawn from the Book of Orders and Rules prepared and enforced by Anthony Maria Brown, Viscount Montague, 1595. According to this rule, only the Clerke of the Kitchen and the Gentleman Usher come close to having this much responsibility.*

1. Make sure provisions are ordered and acquired. This includes beef, mutton, grain, livery badges, wood, coals, wild fowl, wines, salt, hops, spices, fruits of all sorts.
2. Make sure repairs are carried out as needed in any of his lordship's houses, both inside and outside, including

In matters foreign and without the house

maintenance of fences, hedges, marshes, walls, ponds, etc.

3. Distribute wages quarterly to household servants and other manor employees, and provide whatever each one is due in cash or in kind.

4. Deliver money as appropriate to the:
    + Clerke of the Kitchen for purchasing fresh supplies of anything not supplied by the manor.
    + Purveyors of beef and mutton.
    + Gentleman or Yeoman of the Horse for buying feed, equipment, and other necessaries for the stable.
    + Granator for buying wheat or malt, as needed.

5. Collect bills and expense receipts from all these under-officers, review and enter them in his book of accounts (livery book).

6. Ride out into the parks, pastures, marshes, and other grounds to see that they be not abused or disordered, either by his own bailiffs or anyone else.

7. Support the bailiff of Husbandry in his efforts to carry out his lordship's orders.

8. Arrange to sell the hides, skins, horns, wool, and so on of any sheep or oxen slaughtered for the table.

9. Arrange to dispose of the tallow from such sales, keeping part to make candles and rush lights, part for use in the kitchen, and the rest to sell.

10. Get a receipt from anyone to whom money is paid out, all to be filed against the annual audit.

11. Sign-off the livery book for all monies received from his lordship to pay household expenses, each entry to be dated with name of the person paid, location, and nature of the expense.

12. Once a month, report to his lordship with the livery book for review, and once a year to the Auditor.

Scott: "A Book of Orders and Rules"   *Source*

In My Lady's Chamber

THE *chamber* or *bedchamber* is a very public room in a great house; you receive guests there, play cards or chess, and may even dine intimately there with a few close friends. The best bedchamber in the house is the *great chamber.*

If you want some actual privacy, you retire to your *wardrobe* or *closet*—a small, private room off the chamber, used for dressing and other private pursuits such as devotions or letter-writing.

The bed itself is an extravagant affair with embroidered or appliquéd or velvet curtains or *hangings.*

Your bed-clothes include linen or *holland* sheets and woolen blankets with a decorative *coverlet, coverlid* or *counterpane,* and pillows or bolsters. Pillow cases are called *pillow-beres.*

Along with the bed, your chamber is furnished with one or two chairs, some stools, and an assortment of tables and *chests*

The countess of Southampton at her toilette

(wooden storage boxes), all made of good English oak. Your tables may be covered with *Turkey carpets*, if you can afford them. Each stool has its cushion, embroidered by the ladies of the household.

Your valuables—jewels, perfumed gloves, love letters—are kept in various smaller boxes called *coffers* or *caskets*, which might be of precious metal or fine wood, often highly decorated.

The classic dressing-room picture of Elizabeth Vernon, countess to the 3rd Earl of Southampton, shows such a table covering and casket. The other items are jewels and a pin cushion, without which no lady can get dressed.

You probably store your clothing in a *press*, a wooden cupboard with shelves, sometimes with sliding drawers below.

Or you may simply keep clothes in a chest or hang them on pegs. There are no built-in closets with hangers.

At the Sideboard: A Jack & a Gill

A JACK is a waxed leather bottle or tankard such as a huntsman, traveler, or soldier might carry.

Not to be confused with a jack, a stout, metal-studded leather jacket worn by moss troopers, border reivers, and other rowdies.

A *gill* (pronounced "jill") is a measure equal to a quarter of a pint (four ounces), or any cup of this size.

A *pottle* (rhymes with "bottle") is a measure equal to two quarts (half a gallon), or a vessel of this size.

A cup or bowl for soup, broth, and the like is called a *porringer* (po'ran-jer), especially when it has one or two flat han-

A Pottle

dles parallel to the ground. In Northern counties and along the Scottish borders, this is also called a pottinger (pottin-jer).

> Come landlord fill the flowing bowl until it doth run over!
> Come landlord fill the flowing bowl until it doth run over!
> For tonight we'll merry merry be,
>   for tonight we'll merry merry be,
> For tonight we'll merry merry be!
> Tomorrow we'll be sober!

A cup for drinking ale or wine is often called a *pot* or a bowl. (Thus, a drunkard may be called a tosspot.) Call for "a bowl of brown ale" or "a pot of brandywine".

A tapering, cylindrical cup without handles is a *beaker*.

A beaker with three or four evenly-spaced handles is a *tyg* (rhymes with "pig").

A *tankard* is a large drinking cup with a handle.

Plate is all your pewter, silver, or gold dishes, utensils, and

serving pieces collectively. When times are hard, you can always pawn your plate.

When you refer to the plates you use while laying the table, say *dishes* or *trenchers*, as appropriate.

Some good words:

- Leathern—made of leather, as "a leathern jack"
- Treen—made of turned wood (from *tree*), as "a treen platter"

The Steward in Matters Domestical

THE Steward will at all times:

1. Bear himself like the chief officer of a great house.
2. Maintain a submissive and dutiful attitude towards his lordship and his lady and (to a lesser degree) their children, both as his own duty and to set an example to the rest of the staff. Assist his lordship with sound advice and great deliberation, and keep all his secrets.
3. Hire and manage all domestic officers, servants and attendants and, when appropriate, recommend them for advancement (promotion).
4. Be obeyed by every servant and officer in all things whatsoever, no matter how inconvenient, unless the task is dishonest, illegal or harmful to his lordship or his family.
5. Regularly hold a staff meeting of the officers and domestic servants to encourage and remind them of their duties. Remind them that they want to do well for hope of reward and to contribute to both their own and his lordship's credit (good name).

A continuation of the duties laid down in Lord Mopntague's Book of Orders and Rules of 1595

6. Admonish and correct negligent and disordered persons of any degree (both gentlemen and yeomen), and reform them by his grave and vigilant watch over them.
   - He has some discretion in punishments, including suspending them from duties.
   - When he finds them reformed, he can restore them to attendance.
   - Bring the incorrigible and outrageous to his lordship for his direct consideration.
   - No servant is ever to appear before his lordship out of livery.

7. Give appropriate notice if he is going to be away from the house for longer than normal, so the master can find a replacement for the interim.
   - He is not under any circumstances to appoint his own deputy.
   - The deputy will replace him in terms of supervising the household only, not for receipts and payments, because he has to be accountable for those himself.

8. Appoint any of the household to carry messages to neighbors or elsewhere, with these stipulations:
   - Never send a groom of the great chamber or of the wardrobe without informing the Gentleman Usher, or send anyone by horse without informing the Gentleman of the Horse. This is so someone knows where the animal has gone, and so duties can be covered.
   - Get permission in advance before sending any of his lordship's own chamber servants.

9. Share out at his discretion any gifts or rewards (vails) given by guests to the house.

10. Take an inventory of all the plate and silver vessels in the

house, including the weight and type, and goldsmith's mark on each, and make a copy for the Gentleman Usher and another for his lordship.

Scott: "A Book of Orders and Rules"   *Source*

The Oath of a Privy Councillor, 1570

H ERE *is the text of the oath given to every Privy Councillor on his appointment to that office. He swears, his hand upon the Bible.*

You shall swear to be a true and faithful councillor to the Queen's Majesty as one of her Highness's Privy Council.

Sir William Cecil, Lord Burghley

You shall not know or understand any manner of thing to be attempted, done, or spoken against her Majesty's person, honour, crown, or dignity royal but you shall let [resist] and withstand the same to the utmost of your power, and either do or cause it to be forthwith revealed either to her Majesty's self or to the rest of her Privy Council.

You shall keep secret all matters committed and revealed to you as her Majesty's councillor, or that shall be treated of secretly in council.

And if any of the same treaties or counsels shall touch any of the other councillors, you shall not reveal the same to him, but shall keep the same until such time as by consent of her Majesty, or the rest of the Council, publication shall be made thereof.

You shall not let [hesitate] to give true, plain, and faithful counsel at all times, without respect either of the cause or of the person, laying apart all favor, meed [reward], affection, and partiality.

And you shall to your uttermost bear faith and true allegiance to the Queen's Majesty, her heirs and lawful successors, and shall assist and defend all jurisdictions, preeminences, and authorities granted to her Majesty and annexed to her Crown against all foreign princes, persons, prelates, or potentates, whether by act of Parliament or otherwise.

And generally in all things you shall do as a faithful and true councillor ought to do to her Majesty.

So help you God and the holy contents of this Book.

The Great House

The ancient manors and houses of our gentlemen are yet and for the most part of strong timber, in framing whereof our carpenters have been and are worthily preferred before those of like science among all other nations. Howbeit such as be lately builded are commonly either of brick or hard stone, or both,

their rooms large and comely, and houses of office further dis-
tant from their lodgings.

Those of the nobility are likewise wrought with brick and
hard stone, as provision may best be made, but so magnificent
and stately as the basest house of a baron doth often match in
our days with some honours of a prince in old time. So that, if
ever curious building did flourish in England, it is in these our
years wherein our workmen excel and are in manner comparable in skill with old Vitruvius, Leo Baptista, and Serlio.

— *William Harrison*, The Description of England, *1577*

T HE familiar half-timbered Tudor house is becoming
quaint and old-fashioned. If your family is still occupying
a house of this style, it's time to re-design, remodel, or relocate.

Building and remodeling are all the rage—not just pal-
aces and monuments but country houses and even yeoman
farmhouses.

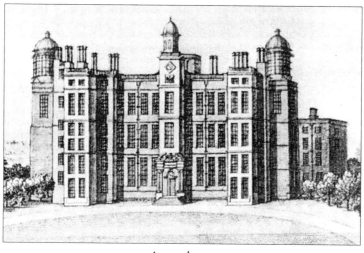

A great house

If you have an ancient family property, you may be adding a new wing with larger chambers and more windows.

If your family is up-and-coming, you may be busy in the land market, acquiring property on which to establish a notable seat suitable to your current dignity. Or you may be modernizing a monastic property acquired by your father or grandfather in the time of Henry VIII.

Those looking for preferment must be prepared to entertain the Queen when she is on Progress—sometimes on a moment's notice. The importance of a commodious Great Chamber, a fashionable dining parlour, and galleries for entertaining and display cannot be over-estimated.

At the same time, knowledge of classical treatises on architecture and continental trends based on them is a sign of your education and taste, and a new or expanded house in the latest fashion is a symbol of your rank and power.

The *stone* for all this building may come from your own quarries, if you have them. Abandoned monasteries often provide dressed stone, timber, and paving tiles, as well as tin and lead for the roof.

Bricks and *tiles* are usually baked on site from local clay.

On window glass   Traditionally, many building elements are thought of as moveable: shutters, doors, window frames, chimney pieces, wainscoting, even staircases. As the great house becomes more of a symbol of family permanence and power, these elements come to be seen as fixtures rather than furnishings.

As late as 1567, glass is thought too fragile for constant use. When you're not in residence, you may instruct the staff to remove the glass panes and place them in storage. They will fill in the space with panels of translucent horn or woven *lattices* fixed into wooden frames.

As glass becomes cheaper, and windows more numerous, they come to be seen as a permanent part of the installation.

With the proliferation of glass, the new houses springing up in the countryside have a tendency to glitter. Happily, no one will think to tax them for another 100 years or so.

The countess of Shrewsbury's great house in Derbyshire indulges the passion for glass to such a degree that people say: *Hardwick Hall, more glass than wall.*

Architecture is a newly revived science, largely promoted in England by Dr. John Dee (1570) and John Shute (1563). It is not a profession but a gentleman's avocation.

On design

> An architect (sayeth Vetruvius) ought to understand languages, to be skillful of painting, well instructed in geometry, not ignorant of perspective, furnished with arithmetic, have knowledge of many histories and diligently have heard philosophers, have skill of music, not ignorant of physic, know the answers of lawyers, and have astronomy and the courses celestial in good knowledge. He giveth reason, orderly, wherefore all these arts, doctrines, and instructions are requisite in an excellent architect.
>
> —*John Dee, 1570*

If you cannot import an architect from Italy, you probably design your new house yourself, with assistance from a *Master Mason, Builder,* or *Carpenter,* with a *Surveyor of the Works* to supervise the workmen.

Some things never change: In 1594, Lady Shrewsbury sought legal redress against a workman who had absented himself from work already begun and paid for.

The principal influences:

- Vitruvius, *Ten Books on Architecture* (1st century Roman)
- Leo Baptista Alberti, *On the Art of Building,* 1435

- Serlio, *On Architecture*, 1537
- John Shute, *The First and Chief Grounds of Architecture*, 1563
- Palladio, *The Four Books of Architecture*, 1570

If like Dr Dee you've been reading the classical authors or the more modern Italians, you understand that the ornamentation of a house should be appropriate to the rank, dignity and style of the people who live in it. Thus, a great lord's house should have more "curious" ornament than a yeoman farmer's house.

Classical ornament includes columns based on modern interpretations of Roman and Greek models, molded terra cotta medallions, and symmetrical facades.

Don't feel obliged to copy anything too closely, however. Even your neighbors are borrowing only the ornamental elements that please them, rather than whole floor plans.

In fact, your new facade may be totally unrelated to the style of the room plan behind it, which is likely still traditional. If you are merely remodeling, you may choose to tack a new facade on to your present but unfashionably medieval building.

> *Propriety arises when buildings having magnificent interiors are provided with elegant entrance courts to correspond; for there will be no propriety in the spectacle of an elegant interior approached by a low, mean entrance.*
>
> — Vitruvius

Sources   Airs: *The Tudor and Jacobean Country House*
Cooper: *Houses of the Gentry*
Orlin: *Elizabethan Households*

A Plan of Ingatestone Hall

INGATESTONE *Hall* was built in brick around 1540 by Sir William Petre (it's pronounced "Peter") on an Essex property called variously "Gynge Abbess" or "Yenge atte Stone", which Petre bought from the Crown in 1539 after the dissolution of the wealthy nunnery of Our Lady and St. Ethelberga of Barking.

A country house of the latter sixteenth century

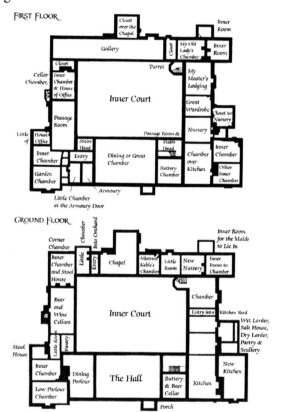

Drawings by Paula Kate Marmor, based on floor plans in Tudor Secretary, *by F.G. Emmison, Harvard, 1961. Post-1600 alterations have been omitted.*

These plans represent the main Hall in the period 1550–1600. Other buildings on the property included a gatehouse, porter's lodge, bake house, brewery, milk-house, stable, mews, slaughterhouse, granary, wash-house, fish-house, still-house, and chambers for the majority of the servants.

A *house of office* is a privy, and a *closet* is any small private room, not necessarily used for storing clothes. Mistress Keble is Sir William's *good mother*, or mother-in-law.

The Hall is still owned and occupied by the Petre family. Portions are open to the public.

Gardens in Season

F RANCIS *Bacon held that "in the royal ordering of gardens there ought to be gardens for all months of the year, in which severally things of beauty may then be in season…" He then recommended these flowering plants and trees from those in season in each month.*

"These particulars are for the climate of London."

The latter part of November, December, January	Such things as are green all winter: Holly, ivy, bays, juniper, cypress trees, yew, pineapple trees, fir trees, rosemary, lavender, periwinkle (white, purple and blue varieties), flags, orange trees, lemon trees, and myrtles (if they be stoved), and sweet marjoram, if warm set.
The latter part of January and Februray	The mezereon tree (daphne) which then blossoms, crocus (both yellow and grey), primroses, anemones, early tulips, hyacinth, charmaris, fritellaria.
March	Violets (especially the single blue), yellow daffodil, daisy, almond tree in blossom, peach tree in blossom, cornelian tree in blossom, sweetbriar.

Rose

Violet (the double white), wall-flower, stock gillyflower, cow-   *April*
slip, flower-de-luce [iris], lilies of all kinds, rosemary flowers,
tulips, double peony, the pale daffodil, French honeysuckle,
cherry tree in blossom, damascene and plum tree in blossom,
white thorn in leaf, the lilac tree.

Pinks [carnations] of all sorts, especially the blush pink;   *May and*
roses of all kinds, except the musk rose which comes later;   *June*
honeysuckle, strawberries, bugloss, columbine, the French
marigold (*flos africanus*, also called African marigold—pretty
but poisonous). Also, cherry tree in fruit, ribes [currants], figs
in fruit, raspberries, vine flowers, lavender in flowers, sweet
satyrion (white), *herba muscaria, lilium convallium*, apple tree in
blossom.

All kinds of gillyflowers, musk roses, the lime tree in blossom,   *July*
early pears and plums in fruit, gentians, quadlins.

Plums of all sorts, pears, apricots, barberries, filberts, musk-   *August*
melons, monks-hoods of all colors.

Grapes, apples, poppies of all colors, wardens, quinces.   *September*

A garden party

October and early November

Services, medlars, bullaces, roses that have been cut or removed (pruned) to come late, hollyoaks, and such like.

And because the breath of flowers is far sweeter in the air (where it comes and goes like the warbling of music) than in the hand, therefore nothing is more fit for that delight, than to know what be the flowers and plants that do best perfume the air.

+ Violets
+ Musk rose
+ Sweetbriar
+ Wall-flowers, which are very delightful to be set under a parlor or lower chamber window.
+ Pinks and gillyflowers, especially the matted pink and clove gillyflower.

- The flowers of the lime-tree.
- Then the honeysuckles, so they be somewhat afar off.

Bacon: *On Gardens*   *Source*

The Hunt is Up

HUNTING is an aristocratic privilege, sport, exercise, social occasion, and a means of putting fresh meat on the table. The Queen is very fond of hunting, as are we all, at whatever early hour and in all weathers.

All men and many women of the upper classes hunt unless prevented by age or infirmity. Very few people are squeamish about hunting, and none but the youngest child is sentimental about the fate of the prey.

The huntsman

The prey The most dangerous prey is the *wild boar*, which is hunted only by men, on foot, with dogs and spears.

The most common prey is *deer*, hunted on horseback and foot.

Venery refers to hunting, and *venison* is any game meat, but usually means specifically the meat of the deer. The words for collections of animals, such as a herd of deer or a set of badgers, are *terms of venery*.

The *red deer* of medieval legend is becoming rare even in the remotest regions. The male is a *hart* or *stag*, and the female is a *hind*. A yearling is a *calf*.

The *fallow deer* is the common deer, and is easiest to hunt. The male is a *buck* and the female is a *doe*.

The *roe deer* is a smaller deer, and is very rare except in old songs.

June is *calving season*. The two weeks either side of midsummer are known as "fence month". To let the deer drop their calves undisturbed, the foresters put up fences at key access points to the forest, and charge a toll to any carts or wagons passing through.

The chase A *forest* is not defined as wild, impenetrable woodland, but rather royal property which has been managed by officials called *foresters* for hundreds of years. Their job is to protect the *vert and venison*—the deer and the plants they rely on for food and cover—for the benefit of the Crown.

In legal terms, even open, unwooded land can be a forest. In the time of King John, all of Essex including towns, villages, and farms was forest.

When the forest is a hunting preserve, it is a *chase*.

Her Majesty at the Hunt

A *park* is a gentleman's private deer reserve. Most great estates have their own attached deer park for the hunting pleasure of the lord and his guests, and to provide fresh meat year-round.

> "A forest must always have beasts of venery abiding in it, otherwise it is no forest: and if there be no beasts of forest, nor beasts of chase in the same, then may men fell their woods that they have within the forest and destroy their covers"
> — John Manwood, *Treatise on the Lawe of the Forests*, 1598

Danziger: *1215, The Year of Magna Carta*   Sources
Pollard: *Imagining Robin Hood*
Whitlock: *Historic Forests of England*
Seeing the Forests for the Trees:
    http://info.sjc.ox.ac.uk/forests/tw.html

The Marriage Ring

THE modern engagement wedding set is unknown, although diamonds are popular. Mary Queen of Scots sent a diamond ring to Thomas duke of Norfolk as a symbol of her willingness to marry him. And Queen Elizabeth gave the duc d'Alencon a diamond ring with a pledge of her hand in marriage.

The ring goes on the third finger of the left hand (ring finger) as it does today. The common belief was that women have a vein in that finger that leads directly to the heart. Even people who know that can't be true believe it at weddings.

Margaret Audley, the duchess of Norfolk, is shown with a simple, if rather large, diamond on the third finger of her left hand.

In 1567, Elizabeth Polsted's wedding ring cost 4 shillings, which included 9d for extra gold.

Mottoes Many marriage rings have mottoes inscribed on the inside or outside of the band, usually in French or Latin. These are usually brief:

Love True

Forever

With everlasting Love

Or they may be longer:

I am yours, love me truly.

After consent, ever content.

Love me and leave me not.

Some may be in Latin, for the loftier minded:

Maneat inviolata fides (Let your faith be inviolate)

Conjugii firmi et casti sum pignus amoris (I am the pledge of loyal marriage and chaste love.)

There are a few variations, including the interlocking *gimmel* or *joint ring*, rather like a puzzle ring. The gimmel consists of from 3 to 8 interlocking bands.

Some versions open to reveal a heart. Some have a motto on each band creating a little poem or *poesy*. These are also called *poesy rings*. For example:

Love is fix'd, I will not range
I like my choice, I will not change
Wit, health, and beauty all do dwell
But constant Love doth far excel

or

The eye do find
The heart doth choose
And love doth bind
Till death doth loose

And so on... Among the poor, many wives may go their whole lives without a ring, due to the cost. (In a country village, everyone knows who is married.) In some families, the ring may be one that has been preserved and passed down.

However, wearing the espousal or marriage ring isn't either universal or sentimental. Many portraits show no ring at all, on men or women.

Although Vives and others praise the wedding ring as a symbol of the bonds of marriage, no one ever offers to explain why men don't wear them. Puritans disapprove of them as intolerable Romish superstition.

Scottish protestants don't use a ring in their ceremonies, and English Puritans resist it furiously.

Widows put away their marriage rings since they are no longer considered to be married.

Sources   Cressy: *Birth, Marriage & Death*
Pearson: *Elizabethans at Home*
Kuntz: *Rings for the Finger*

More Christmas Revels

I N many homes, they play *flapdragon* or *snapdragon*. You take turns picking raisins out of a dish of flaming brandy and popping them into your mouth. Try not to get burnt! Wager on each person's chances of success.

On *Christmas Eve*, girls play fortune-telling games, especially hoping to divine who they will marry.

Ordinary rural people enjoy feasting, dancing, card playing, carol singing, storytelling, party games like *hot cockles* and *shoe-*

ing the mare and attempting to bit an apple with a candle stuck in it hung on a string from the end of a stick.

Christmas *carols* are mainly associated with Christmas Eve   *Caroling* and morning, often performed by the town waits (musicians hired by the town).

Originally a carol was a song to accompany a ring dance for men and women, holding hands. The word acquired its current meaning sometime in the 15th century. They are never sung (or danced) in church.

Most carols are about the nativity, but may also be generally devotional. Others can even be satiric, amorous, or funny!

Musicians and carollers visit the principal houses in the parish, in ascending order of importance. Householders are expected to reward them with a penny, cider, cakes, and so on.

Caroling is intimately associated with wassailing, which is mainly performed by young men.

Wassailing involves blessing the land, especially apple groves,   *Wassailing* and livestock with cider. In Kent, groups of young men make a round of the orchards, performing the rite for a reward.

In the towns, groups of girls and boys go round the neighborhood with a be-ribboned but empty drinking cup or bowl begging for the master of each house to fill it with spiced ale to drink his health, or with cakes, or cheese, or a silver penny. It's bad luck for the host to decline.

Wassailing outings are also a holiday diversion among the gentry. Great county families often have wassail cups of considerable value, which they preserve and pass down as an heirloom. However, the custom has not been followed at Court since old King Henry's time.

When someone greets you with a cheery "Wassail!" you should reply "Drink hail!"

Lord of   All "persons of worship" including Lieutenants and Sheriffs of
Misrule   counties, and even bishops, appoint a Lord of Misrule to manage the merriment of the Twelve Days.

At the inns of court and at the universities, Misrule is usually elected on St Thomas's Day, so there is plenty of time to
plan. He then chooses officers for his Court of Misrule such
as Marshal, Master of the Game, Constable, and Chief Butler. For Christmas 1561, the Lord of Misrule at the Inner Temple was Lord Robert Dudley.

On each of the twelve days of Christmas, his rule runs from
evening until breakfast the next day. His duties consist consist-
ing mainly of presiding over the feasting, games, and dancing.

At supper, the courtiers of Misrule are cried in to the hall
with silly names like Sir Francis Flatterer, Sir Randall Raka-
bite of Rascall Hall in the County of Rakehell, Sir Morgan
Mumchance, or Sir Bartholomew Balbreech of Buttocksbury.
All very Blackadder.

Twelfth   The day begins, like Christmas, with a dramatic religious serv-
Day and   ice featuring the coming of the Three Kings. It had become
Night   traditional for the king to make offerings at Mass of gold,
frankincense & myrrh to symbolize his connection with those
kings and with Christ. This custom survived the Reformation.

The festivities are the most sumptuous of the year, filled with
royal balls and parties.

For Twelfth Day and Night among less exalted folk, a bean
is baked into a cake and pieces distributed among the children
and servants.

Whoever finds the bean is pronounced *King of the Bean*, and reigns for the rest of the day and night. If a pea is used as well, whoever finds it becomes (or chooses) the Queen of the Pea.

Hutton: *Stations of the Sun*   *Sources*
Hubert: *Christmas in Shakespeare's England*
Machyn: *Diary*
Strong & Oman: *The English Year*

A London & Westminster Directory

Nᴏᴛ every nobleman needs or wants to keep a house in London. In the 1570s and '80s, these are some of those who do.

House	Nobleman	District in London
Arundel	Henry Fitzalan, earl of Arundel	Arundel House, the Strand
Bacon	Sir Nicholas Bacon	York House, the Strand
Burghley	William Cecil, lord Burghley	Burghley House, the Strand
Derby	Henry Stanley, earl of Derby	Derby House, Canon Row
Effingham	Charles Howard, lord Howard of Effingham	Kings Street, Westminster
Hatton	Sir Christopher Hatton	Ely Place, Holborn
Hertford	Edward Seymour, earl of Hertford	Hertford House, Canon row

House	Nobleman	District in London
Hunsdon	Henry Carey, lord Hunsdon	King's Place, Hackney (technically out-of-town, Hackney is north of the city)
Leicester	Robert Dudley, earl of Leicester	Leicester House, the Strand
Lincoln	Henry Clinton, earl of Lincoln	Lincoln House, Canon row
Lumley	John Lumley, lord Lumley	Crutched Friars, Tower Hill
Oxford	Edward deVere, earl of Oxford	Oxford Court, London Stone; Fishers Folly, Bishopsgate
Pembroke	Henry Herbert, earl of Pembroke	Baynard's Castle, Blackfriars
Ralegh	Sir Walter Ralegh	Durham House, the Strand
South-ampton	Henry Wriothesley, earl of Southampton	Drury Place, the Barbican
South-ampton	Mary, dowager countess of Southampton	Southampton House, Chancery Lane
Sussex	Thomas Radcliffe, earl of Sussex	Sussex House, Canon Row
Willough-by	Peregrine Bertie, lord Willoughby d'Eresby	Willoughby House, the Barbican

God Save the Queen

F ROM *Annals of the first four years of the reign of Queen Elizabeth*, Sir John Hayward, 1599

Now, if ever any person had either the gift or the style to win the hearts of people, it was this Queen. And if ever she did express the same, it was at that present, in coupling mildness with majesty as she did, and in stately stooping to the meanest sort. All her faculties were in motion, and every motion seemed a well-guided action. Her eye was set upon one, her care listened to another, her judgment upon a third, to a fourth she addressed her speech. Her spirit seemed to be everywhere, and yet so entire in herself, as it seemed to be nowhere else.

Some she pitied, some she commended, some she thanked, at others she pleasantly and wittily jested, condemning no person, neglecting no office, and distributing her smiles, looks, and graces so artfully that thereupon the people again redoubled the testimonies of their joys. And afterwards, raising eve-

The Queen removes herself from Hatfield to London, November 18, 1558

Her Grace with a lute

rything to the highest strain, filled the ears of all men with immoderate extolling their Prince.

Of her personal appear-ance and character

She was a lady upon whom nature had bestowed and well placed many of her fairest favors: of stature mean, slender, straight, and amiably disposed; of such state in her carriage as every motion of her seemed to bear majesty. Her hair was inclined to pale yellow, her forehead large and fair, her eyes lively and sweet but short-sighted, her nose somewhat rising in the middle, the whole compass of her countenance somewhat long yet of admirable beauty, not so much in that which is termed the flower of youth, as in a most delightful composition of majesty and modesty in equal mixture.

But without good qualities of mind, the gifts of nature are like painted flowers, without either virtue or sap; yea, sometimes they grow horrid and loathsome. Now her virtues were such as might suffice to make an Ethiope beautiful, which the more a man knows and understands, the more he shall admire and love. In life, she was most innocent; in desires, moderate; in purpose, just; of spirit, above credit and almost capacity of her sex; of divine wit, as well for depth of judgment, as for quick conceit and speedy expedition; of eloquence, as sweet in the utterance, so ready and easy to come to the utterance: of wonderful knowledge, both of learning and affairs; skillful not only in the Latin and Greek but also in other diverse foreign languages.

None knew better, the hardest art of all others, that is, of commanding men, nor could more use themselves to those cares without which the royal dignity could not be supported. She was religious, magnanimous, merciful, and just; respective of the honour of others, and exceeding tender in the touch of her own.

She was lovely and loving, the two principal bands of duty and obedience. She was very ripe and measured in counsel and experience, as well not to let go occasions as not to take them when they were green.

Excellent Queen! What do my words but wrong thy worth? What do I but gild gold? What but show the sun with a candle, in attempting to praise thee, whose honour doth fly over the whole world upon the two wings of Magnanimity and Justice, whose perfection shall much dim the luster of all other that shall be of thy sex?

Bonus: Character Questions for Courtiers (and others)

THIS list assumes a sizeable group of people meeting each week with a leader or director to work on character development for Court, but of course it can be adapted for any needs.

Each session begins with each person saying their name, and answering a standard question that usually changes every week (see #1, Introductions). The facilitator may ask for elaboration on any answer, and leave room for discussion, if appropriate. The last thing of the evening is that everyone in turn gets to ask one question of anyone else in the room. Collect any really good ones and add them to the list!

The only wrong answer is: "I don't know."

Because this exercise is designed to teach you about everyone else, as well as about yourself, it's a good idea to write down your own and others' answers. I once asked a maid of honour what sort of presents she liked, so when I wanted a favor, I would know how to sweeten my request!

Ready...Go!

1. Introductions: Who are you and (one of the following):

  • Where were you born?
  • What is your religion?
  • Who are your parents?
  • Who are your siblings?
  • What near relatives are travelling with you?
  • Why are you here?
  • When did you first come to Court?
  • What is the first thing you'll do on the day they make *you* Queen?

2. Give a 1- or 2-word response to:

- marriage
- family
- my greatest flaw
- my greatest virtue (or asset)
- my overall character
- etc.

3. What is more important: Lineage (blood/family/inheritance) or Accomplishment?

4. To whom do you look for guidance?

5. Describe a good servant.

6. What makes a good marriage (remember to think period)?

7. What should one look for in a husband (wife)?

8. Something very few people know about you (or would be surprised to learn).

9. What is the most virtuous thing you have ever done?

10. Why have you come to Court?

11. What really ticks you off?

12. What is a question you would prefer not to answer?

13. Of what ancestor or relative are you most proud (or embarrassed)?

14. What person in your life are you most proud to know (or to have known)?

15. Who is your best friend? Your most useful?

16. What is something you know that gives you an advantage over someone?

17. When you have money, what do you like to spend it on?

18. What does God want? How do you know?

19. Who is the most virtuous person you know?

20. Who is the most sinful person you know?

21. What is the most important thing your father taught you? Your mother?

22. Give a one word response to:

    • religion (the concept not the name of your church)
    • your father's character
    • the nature of nobility

23. Who (if anyone) depends on you for protection, advice, etc.

24. How did you spend your last birthday (even if you didn't celebrate it)?

25. Give advice to a person just coming to Court.

26. What do you like best about being noble? (Or, what do you think would be the best thing about being noble?)

27. What would you like your epitaph to be?

28. What is your greatest fear?

29. How do you think you are perceived by others (whether or not you care)?

30. What kind of person do you think you are?

31. If you were to ask the Queen for something, what would it be?

32. Who is someone who needs to be taught a lesson/put in their place?

33. Describe a happy family.

34. How do you deal with a rival?

35. What is the highest virtue?

36. What is the greatest shame?

37. When you go home, where do you go?

38. Where do you prefer to live: in the city or the countryside?

39. What is your favorite anecdote about the Queen?

40. What is the most amusing thing you can recall happening on Progress?

41. How did you spend last Christmas?

42. What is the value of educating women?

43. What would you do with £1,000?

44. What is the most have you ever risked on a single wager?

45. When you want the latest gossip, who do you ask?

46. When you have just learned something juicy/important, who do you tell first?

47. What is your favorite oath?

48. What item do you feel naked without?

49. How sensitive are you to remarks about:

- your mother
- your religion
- your courage
- something in your past
- your sex life

50. Ask yourself a question: What is something you think is significant about you that we haven't asked for?

Final exam   Tell something you know about everyone in the room, in turn.

NOTE: These questions are based on a list initially developed for St. George's Guild (South) by Bob and Margie Wright, enlarged by Athene Mihalakis. With help from the rest of the cast, the list grew over numerous Wednesday night rehearsals facilitated by Lloyd Winter and myself. They are available for anyone to use and modify as they like.

Bibliography & Resources

THIS *is not an attempt at an exhaustive bibliography. Rather, it is a decent reading list which happens to include most of the* (printed) *sources of this book.*

Airs, Malcolm, *The Tudor and Jacobean Country House: A Building History*, Sutton, 1995.

Bacon, Francis, "On Gardens", in *Essays or Counsels, Civil and Moral*, 1597.

Berleth, Richard, *The Twilight Lords, an Irish Chronicle*, Alfred A. Knopf, New York, 1978; rpt. Barnes and Noble, 1994.

Boutell's Heraldry, revised by J.P Brooke-Little (Richmond Herald of Arms), Frederick Warne & Co., Ltd., London, 1950; rev. 1970.

Briggs, Asa, *A Social History of England*, Viking Press, New York, 1983.

Burgess, Anthony, *Shakespeare*, Penguin Books, London, 1970.

Chappell, William, *The Ballad Literature and Popular Music of the Olden Time*, vol. 1. (Dover reprint)

Cole, Mary Hill, *The Portable Queen: Elizabeth I and the Politics of Ceremony*, University of Mass. Press, 1999.

Cooper, Nicholas, *Houses of the Gentry, 1480–1680*, Yale, 1999.

Cressy, David, *Birth, Marriage, and Death: Ritual, Religion, and the Life-Cycle in Tudor and Stuart England*, Oxford University Press, 1997.

Daiches, David and John Flower, *Literary Landscapes of the British Isles*, Paddington Press, Ltd., New York, 1979.

Danziger, Danny, *1215: The Year of Magna Carta*, Touchstone, New York, 2004.

Dawson, Giles E. and Laetitia Kennedy-Skipton, *Elizabethan Handwriting, 1500–1650, A Manual*, W.W. Norton & Co., New York, 1966.

Derrick, John, *An Image of Irland*, 1585.

The Diary of Henry Machyn, John Gough Nichols, ed., Camden Society Old Series, 1848, (rpt. AMS Press, 1968).

Dovey, Zillah, *An Elizabethan Progress: The Queen's Journey into East Anglia, 1578*, Sutton, 1996.

Duffy, Eamon, *The Voices of Morebath: Reformation & Rebellion in an English Village*, Yale, 2001.

Dunn, Jane, *Elizabeth and Mary: Cousins, Rivals, Queens*, Alfred A. Knopf, 2004.

Emerson, Kathy, *Wives and Daughters, Women of 16th Century England*, Whitson Publishing Co., New York, 1984.

Emmison, F.G., *Tudor Secretary: Sir William Petre at Court and Home*, Longmans, London, 1987.

Epstein, Norrie, *The Friendly Shakespeare*, Viking, New York, 1993.

Erickson, Carolly, *The First Elizabeth*, Summit Books, New York, 1983.

Fox-Davies, Arthur Charles, *A Complete Guide to Heraldry*, Bonanza Books, New York, 1978.

Fraser, Antonia, *Mary Queen of Scots*, Delacorte Press, New York, 1969.

Fraser, George MacDonald, *The Steel Bonnets*, Pan Books, London, 1971.

Grimal, Pierre, *The Dictionary of Classical Mythology*, trans. A.R. Maxwell, Basil Blackwell, Inc., New York, 1966.

Gristwood, Sarah, *Elizabeth & Leicester: Power, Passion, Politics*, Viking, 2007.

Harrison, William, *Description of Elizabethan England 1577*, rpt. Kessinger Publishing, 2008.

Hayward's Annals of Elizabeth, Camden Society Old Series, 1840; rpt. AMS Press, 1968.

Hibbert, Christopher, *The English: A Social History, 1066–1945*, Grafton Books, W.W. Norton & Co., New York, 1987.

Hubert, Maria, *Christmas in Shakespeare's England*, Sutton, 1998.

Hutton, Ronald, *Stations of the Sun, A History of the Ritual Year in Britain*, Oxford, 1995.

Jones, Norman, *The Birth of the Elizabethan Age: England in the 1560s*, Blackwell Publishers, Oxford, 1993.

Kuntz, George Frederick, *Rings for the Finger*, 1917; rpt., Dover Books, New York, 1973.

Lacey, Robert, *Robert, Earl of Essex: an Elizabethan Icarus*, Redwood Press, Ltd., 1971.

Laning, Chris, "Faire Names for English Folk: Late Sixteenth Century English Names", 2000. http://www.s-gabriel .org/names/christian/fairnames/ (accessed 2007)

The Lisle Letters, Muriel St. Clare Byrne, ed., selected and arranged by Bridget Boland, Univ. of Chicago Press, 1983.

Loades, David, *The Tudor Court*, Barnes & Noble, New Jersey, 1987.

Love, Dr. Ronald, workshops and discussions, 1980–83.

The Maryknoll Catholic Dictionary, ed. Albert J. Nevins, Grosset & Dunlop, New York, 1965.

Mattingly, Garrett, *The Armada*, Houghton Mifflin, 1959.

Monson, Shelly, "Elizabethan Holiday Customs", 1998. http:// guildofstgeorge.com/holiday.htm (accessed 2006–2008).

Morrison, Fynes, *Itineraries*, 1617.

Orlin, Lena Cowen, *Elizabethan Households*, Folger Shake-speare Library, 1995.

New Oxford English Dictionary (compact edition), Oxford University Press, 1971.

The Oxford Illustrated History of Britain, Kenneth O. Morgan, ed., Oxford University Press, 1984.

Pearson, Lu Emily, *Elizabethans at Home*, Stanford University Press, 1957.

Plowden, Allison, *The Elizabethan Secret Service*, St. Martin's, 1991.

Pollard, A. J., *Imagining Robin Hood*, 2004.

Pritchard, Ron, *Shakespeare's England: Life in Elizabethan and Jacobean Times*, Sutton, 2000.

The Renaissance in England, Hyder E. Rollins & Herschel Baker, eds., D.C Heath & Co., 1954.

Rowse, A.L. *The England of Elizabeth: The Structure of Society*, The University of Wisconsin Press, 1978.

————*The Elizabethan Renaissance: The Life of the Society*, Charles Scribner's Sons, New York, 1971.

————*Shakespeare's Southampton: Patron of Virginia*, Harper & Row, New York, 1965.

————*Sir Walter Ralegh: His Family and Private Life*, Harper & Bros., New York, 1962.

Sass, Lorna J. *To the King's Taste*, Metropolitan Museum of Art, St. Martin's Press, New York, 1975.

————*To the Queen's Taste*, Metropolitan Museum of Art, St. Martin's Press, New York, 1976.

Rubel, William, Correspondence, April 2007. (http://www.williamrubel.com/artisanbread)

Scott, A.F., *The Tudor Age*, Thomas Y. Crowell Company, New York, 1975.

Scott, Sir Sibbald David, "A Book of Orders and Rules", in *Sussex Archaeological Collections*, vol. vii, London, 1854.

Shakespeare's World: Background Readings in the English Renaissance, Gerald M. Pinciss & Roger Lockyer, eds., Continuum Publishing, New York, 1989.

Smith, Alan G. R., *Servant of the Cecils: The Life of Sir Michael Hicks 1543–1612*, Jonathon Cape, 1977.

Smith, Lacey Baldwin, *The Elizabethan World*, Houghton Mifflin, 1972.

Somerset, Anne, *Ladies in Waiting, from the Tudors to the Present Day*, Alfred A. Knopf New York, 1984.

Speed, John, *The Counties of Britain, A Tudor Atlas*, Thames & Hudson, (in assoc. with The British Library) 1988; maps orig. published in 1611–12.

Stone, Lawrence, *The Crisis of the Aristocracy 1558–1641*, Clarendon Press, 1965.

——*Family and Fortune: Studies in Aristocratic Finance*, Clarendon Press, 1973.

Stopes, C. C., *The Life of Henry 3rd Earl of Southampton, Shakespeare's Patron*, 1922.

Stowe, John, *A Survey of London ...*, *1598*, Henry Morely, ed., Sutton, 1997.

Strong, Roy, *Gloriana: The Portraits of Queen Elizabeth I*, Thames and Hudson, 1987.

Strong, Roy and Julia Trevelyan Oman, *The English Year*, Ticknor & Fields, New York 1982.

Stubbes, Philip, *The Anatomie of Abuses*, Margaret Jane Kidnie, ed., Renaissance English Text society, 2002.

Tudor Constitution, Documents and Commentary, The, G. R. Elton, ed.., Cambridge University Press, 2nd ed, 1982.

Whitlock, R., *Historic Forests of England*, 1979.

Williams, Neville, *All the Queen's Men*, Macmillan, New York 1972.

Williams, Penry, *The Later Tudors, England 1547–1603*, Oxford University Press, 1995.

——*The Tudor Regime*, Clarendon Press, Oxford, 1979.

Young, Alan, *Tudor and Jacobean Tournaments*, Sheridan House, 1987.

Topics by Category

THE chapters of the *Compendium* are arranged to make accessing history easy and painless. But sometimes you do need to focus your reading on a particular topic. This list groups chapters into broad categories for your convenience.

Numbers & Measures, Dates & Time *What*
Money *counts*
At the Sideboard: A Jack and a Gill
More Measures
Random Bits & Bobs

Religion *Religion*
Comparative Religion: Roman Catholics
Comparative Religion: The Church of England
More Comparative Religion: Calvinists
More Religion
Virtue and Vice, or vice versa

Love and Marriage *Love and*
Betrothal & Wedding *marriage*
More Wedding Customs
The Marriage Ring

Language: Thee & Thou *Using the*
More Language: Mishandled Words *language*
More Language: Some random vocabulary
Still More Language: Alternatives
A Fashionable Vocabulary: Clothing and Fabrics
More Fashionable Vocabulary

Social Titles and Forms of Address
relationships Masters & Servants
Patronage: Retinue, Companions & Livery
Greasing the Wheels
Ranks & Files
Precedence, Preferment & Attainder
The Senior Peers of England
The Noble Style
Honour and Dueling
Forms of Address for Common Folk
Staffing a Great Household

Work and Services and Occupations
play More Services and Occupations
Games
Filling the Time
More Things To Do
Still More Things To Do
The Hunt is Up
Letter Writing

Domestic Domestic Details
concerns Of Bread & Wine
The City of London
Household Management
Paying the Servants
Science and Health (without key to the scriptures)
What We Eat
Food & Your Life Style
More of What We Eat
Snack Foods

Dinner at Cowdray House, 1595
Good English Ale
To Set a Fine Table
The Steward and His Office
The Steward in Matters Domestical
In My Lady's Chamber
The Great House
Plan of Ingatestone Hall
Gardens in Season
A London & Westminster Directory

Ireland   *Political*
Scotland   *discourse*
Mary Queen of Scots (1542–1587) An incredibly brief account
Shopping in London
Spain, France, Germany, Italy & other despicable places
The Queen's Suitors: The Short List
The Royal Sweepstakes
The Oath of a Privy Councillor, 1570
God Save the Queen

Children & Childhood   *Children*
Heirs & Inheritance   *and*
Naming the Baby   *education*
Proverbs & Wise Sayings
What Every Schoolboy Knows
Classical References
A Classical Education

Keeping Christmas   *Christmas*
Gifts at the New Year   *revels*
More Christmas Revels

Index

glass 150
gods 112
good works 21, 57
grace through sacraments 21
grammar school 111
granator 140
grasshopper 71
greasing the wheels 34
great chamber 141
Greek & Roman gods 112
Greenwich Palace 129
Gresham, Sir Thomas 71
Grey, Lady Catherine 92
Grocers Company 118
grooms 29

H

Hampton Court 129
handicraftmen 77
hangings 141
Hapsburg, Archduke Charles 89
Hardwick Hall 151
Harrington, Sir John 108
Hastings, Henry, earl of Huntington 93
Hatton, Sir Christopher 55, 91
Hawkins, Sir John 55
head of the Church 21
Hebrew 36
heiress 85
heirs to the throne 91
Heneage, Sir Thomas 91
Henry VIII 68, 91
Henslow's Diary 117
heraldry 86
Herbert, Mary (Sidney), countess of Pembroke 104
herbs 39

heresy 19
Highlands 67
holland 141
holly and ivy 129
Holy Roman Empire 81
honey 36, 62, 79, 137
honor 55
horn in place of windows 150
hose 74
hospitality 129
household 107, 129, 139
House of Lords 49
house of office 154
Howard. Thomas, duke of Norfolk 91
Huguenots 81
humours 62
hunting 157
husbandmen 77, 96

I

income 54
indulgences 21, 24
infidelity 19
Ingatestone Hall 153
Inner Temple 164
Ireland 64

J

jack 143
James VI 93
Jesuits 13
jewelers 72
jointure 17, 19, 127

K

kitchens at Court 97
knights 26, 48, 75
Knollys, Lettyce 89

About the Author

MAGGIE Secara was for many years the Countess of Southampton in the Guild of St. George at the Renaissance Pleasure Faire (California). She has also been active in Clan MacColin and the Kriegshunde Fähnlein, and directed both performance and costume. In the Society for Creative Anachronism, she is Mistress Máirghrèad-Rós FitzGarret of Desmond (O.L.) where for three years she edited *Tournaments Illuminated*, the quarterly journal of the Society.

A technical writer by trade, Maggie has a Master's degree from California State University, Northridge. She and her very understanding husband live with their cats in cozy suburban splendor in North Hollywood, California.

Breinigsville, PA USA
15 February 2010
232520BV00004B/32/P